POCKET
DICTIONARY

FOR THE STUDY OF
BIBLICAL HEBREW

TODD J. MURPHY

InterVarsity Press
Downers Grove, Illinois

InterVarsity Press
P.O. Box 1400, Downers Grove, IL 60515-1426
World Wide Web: www.ivpress.com
E-mail: mail@ivpress.com

InterVarsity Press® is the book-publishing division of InterVarsity Christian Fellowship/USA®, a
student movement active on campus at hundreds of universities, colleges and schools of nursing in the
United States of America, and a member movement of the International Fellowship of Evangelical
Students. For information about local and regional activities, write Public Relations Dept., InterVarsity
Christian Fellowship/USA, 6400 Schroeder Rd., P.O. Box 7895, Madison, WI 53707-7895, or visit the
IVCF website at <www.ivcf.org>.

All Scripture quotations, unless otherwise indicated, are the author's own translation.

Cover design: Cindy Kiple

Cover image: Ed Honowitz/Getty Images

ISBN 0-8308-1458-2

Printed in the United States of America ∞

Library of Congress Cataloging-in-Publication Data

Murphy, Todd J., 1970-
    Pocket dictionary for the study of biblical Hebrew/Todd J. Murphy.
        p. cm.
    ISBN 0-8308-1458-2 (pbk.)
    1. Hebrew language—Grammar—Dictionaries. 2. Hebrew
language—Lexicography—Dictionaries. 3. Bible. O.T.—Language,
style—Dictionaries. I. Title.
    PJ4554.M87 2003
    492.4'3231—dc21

                                                                              2003010920

P	16	15	14	13	12	11	10	9	8	7	6	5	4	3	2
Y	16	15	14	13	12	11	10	09	08	07	06					

To my grandparents,
Vance and Marjorie Oakes,
for your faithfulness and commitment

CONTENTS

Preface

Biblical Hebrew is an exciting and enriching venture for the student of the humanities. Its study draws people together from a variety of fields, such as ministry, theology, linguistics, Bible teaching, ancient Near Eastern studies and those with a general interest in Judaica. Because of the advances in the scientific study of history and language, we are learning more now about Biblical Hebrew (BH) than ever before. However, with the proliferation of these disciplines and their application to the study of BH, there has also developed an ever-enlarging technical vocabulary. While such vocabulary terms are initially intended to define concepts with greater clarity and simplicity, this jargon often grows into a ten-headed hydra standing between the language and the student. This *Pocket Dictionary* has grown out of a personal desire not only to help the student slay this dragon but also generally to make the study of BH more accessible and enjoyable.

The methodological approach to the work is pragmatic. The selection of terms was based on a principle of "encountered" vocabulary. Simply put, those terms that the beginning student of BH is likely to encounter in foundational and intermediate studies have been included. In the study of BH, new terms are constantly being coined as others are being retired. Because of this, an effort has been made to indicate words that represent the preferred nomenclature as well as those words that have generally passed from usage. While such judgments are continually being made by experts, standard tools remain in print with the vocabulary of their respective authors. This *Pocket Dictionary* retains terms that are found in standard grammars and reference works still being used by students in spite of the fact that a more recent nomenclature is often preferred among Hebrew scholars. Thus this work should not be viewed as a "prescribed" vocabulary but rather a descriptive vocabulary aimed at just defining terms as they are used in their particular reference contexts.

In composing this volume, limitations and boundaries had to be set. Thus a couple of considerations should be kept in mind. First, I have attempted a thorough search of the various English introductory works in order to define as much of the basic terminology as possible. Compound terms, which are common, often are defined as a separate entry. Second, I have sought to deal somewhat preemptively with the linguistic and literary disciplines. The research and literature in these fields, especially modern linguistic theory, is growing rapidly. A great deal of this terminology is already found in the literature of the scientific study of BH and the Semitic languages. Therefore I have included some of the fundamental concepts of theoretical linguistics that the student may encounter in venturing into these disciplines.

I have aimed at a brevity as well as sufficiency in the definitions. Where possible and appropriate, an example has been given to aid the student in grasping the concept. In the case of terms that are not peculiar to BH or Semitic languages, examples may be given in English. Where grammatical or linguistic concepts are peculiar to BH, examples are given in BH with an English translation.

A large number of common English grammatical terms have been defined as well. Students entering universities and seminaries in the English-speaking world are generally not as proficient in basic English grammar as were previous generations. So profound is this problem, many seminary professors today are beginning classes in Greek and Hebrew with a review of English grammar. For this reason I have included the most universal and rudimentary terminology as well.

In defining terms it becomes evident that there are often several, and at times many, terms that refer to the same concept. In general, this work has sought to provide one definition that is found under the term most commonly used. Related or synonymous terms are then cross-referenced to this entry. However, some terms possess particular nuances or are used nearly as often as others. In such cases, definitions have been provided for each, though they are still cross-referenced to each other.

One helpful aspect of this volume is the insertion of reference codes to some of the major BH reference grammars. These codes provide a quick reference to other authoritative sources, which will provide further clarification for the student. The works selected for this role are editions that are by definition reference works and have also become the most commonly used standards in the English speaking world. Admittedly, other works could have been employed along with the four chosen, but on the basis of their authority and availability it was determined that these four would suffice.

Finally, graduate students in biblical studies, Semitic languages and theology ought to have other tools at their fingertips to take them beyond this work. A great place to start is the other works in this series, such as the *Pocket Dictionary for the Study of New Testament Greek*, the *Pocket Dictionary of Biblical Studies* and the *Pocket Dictionary of Theological Terms*.

Special thanks must be given to the various people who have in some way contributed to this work. First and foremost, appreciation is due to Dr. Dennis Magary who implanted in my mind the idea for this work when I was a beginning Hebrew student. One summer day in 1996, while sitting in his office, I asked if such a work existed. In response he laughed and said, "No, but if you can come up with one, you can surely get it published!" Thanks should also go to my other Hebrew professors, Richard Averbeck, Ray Ortlund Jr., David M. Howard and Willem VanGemeren. I also want to express my gratitude to those who have given me feedback on the work or encouraged me along the way: Mark Vanderhart, Eugene Merrill, John Long, Alan Groves, Scott Hahn and especially Jim Weaver. I want to thank IVP for including my work in this series and Dan Reid for both his patience and his editorial wisdom. And I wish to thank Bob Buller for his professionalism and expertise in Hebrew, which helped to strengthen the manuscript. Finally, thanks to my wife, Christine, and four boys (Judah, Anson, Keegan and Aiden), and also to my mother, Jean Murphy, whose faith is a constant source of encouragement. This work could not have happened without the support of all these mentioned. All of its shortcomings are mine.

Todd J. Murphy
Providence, Rhode Island, July 2003

How to Use This Pocket Dictionary

Cross-References

This pocket dictionary is cross-referenced using the following system:

An asterisk before a term or phrase indicates that it appears elsewhere in the book as a separate entry. Within an entry, only the first occurrence of a term or phrase is cross-referenced. When two related terms occur with the same phrase, the more specific term or phrase is cross-referenced.

See also references within or at the end of a definition are followed by the name of another entry that provides additional information.

An alphabetized entry title with no definition is followed by *see* and the name of the entry under which the definition will be found.

Grammar Referencing System

This work includes reference codes to four major reference grammars for Biblical Hebrew. These codes will allow students to gain quick and easy access to fuller explanations of concepts defined in this dictionary plus many more examples. The abbreviations and their respective works are as follows:

Joüon   Joüon, P. *A Grammar of Biblical Hebrew.* Translated and revised by T. Muraoka. 2 vols. Subsidia Biblica 14/1–2. Rome: Pontifical Biblical Institute, 1991.

IBHS   Waltke, Bruce K., and Michael O'Connor. *An Introduction to Biblical Hebrew Syntax.* Winona Lake, Ind.: Eisenbrauns, 1990.

GKC   Kautzsch, E., ed. *Gesenius' Hebrew Grammar.* Translated by A. E. Cowley. 2nd ed. Oxford: Oxford University Press, 1910.

MNK   Merwe, Christo H. J. van der, Jackie A. Naudé, and Jan H. Kroeze. *A Biblical Hebrew Reference Grammar.* Biblical Lan-

> guages: Hebrew 3. Edited by Stanley E. Porter and Richard S.
> Hess. Sheffield: Sheffield Academic Press, 1999.

Each of these grammars has its own internal outlining system, which we
have utilized in the references. This will dramatically reduce the time
students must spend looking up information since they may bypass the
table of contents and indexes and turn directly to the outlined section of
the work. The following is an example of what the student will encounter in the work.

> **construct state.** In the Semitic languages in general, the joining of
> nouns into a *genitival relationship by the use of *juxtaposition
> and a *linking condition. Such linking conditions are created usu-
> ally by *proclisis and vowel reduction. There may be from two to
> four words participating in the formation of a construct chain.
> The last word of the chain is always in the *absolute state (e.g.,
> בֵּית דָּוִד "house of David"). Joüon §§92, 129; MNK §§25.1-26.2;
> GKC §§89, 128; *IBHS* §9.

One of the above abbreviations is given first to point the student to a
particular grammar. For example, *IBHS* directs the student to Waltke
and O'Connor's *An Introduction to Biblical Hebrew Syntax*. These are followed by the § symbol, which indicates a numbered section followed by
its respective number. Two of these symbols in a row (§§) indicate that
the subject area is covered in more than one section, which are also referenced. The numbering may also indicate subsections (e.g., 25.1). Some
works, such as GKC, will also use letters for further subdivisions. Serious students are encouraged to employ all of these works. Once they
have familiarized themselves with the respective outlining systems,
they will be able to use the reference codes efficiently.

Abbreviations

abbr.	abbreviation
adj.	adjective
Akk.	Akkadian
BA	Biblical Aramaic
BH	Biblical Hebrew
C	consonant
e.g.	"for example"
Fr.	French
Gk.	Greek
i.e.	"in other words"
Lat.	Latin
MS, MSS	manuscript, manuscripts
MT	Masoretic Text
n.	noun
pl.	plural
sing.	singular
v.	verb
V	vowel

A

aabb patterning. *See* patterning.

abab patterning. *See* patterning.

abba patterning. Also known as *chiasm. *See* patterning.

Abisha Scroll. *n.* The most sacred copy of the *Samaritan Pentateuch in the community at Shechem. The older section comprises Numbers 35—Deuteronomy 34 and is dated to approximately the twelfth century A.D.

ablative. *adj.* A noun or pronoun that expresses instrumentality or deprivation (i.e., from, or away from).

ablaut. *See* apophony.

absolute case. *See casus pendens.*

absolute degree. *See* positive degree; degree.

absolute infinitive. *See* infinitive absolute.

absolute nominative. *See casus pendens.*

absolute noun. *n.* (1) A *casus pendens* construction that thus has no grammatical relationship to the sentence; (2) the absolute noun of a construct relationship.

absolute object. *See* cognate accusative.

absolute state. *n.* A word following a construct noun in BH and the Semitic languages is considered to be in the absolute state. The two words are joined by a *linking condition to form a *genitival relationship where both convey one idea, such as בֵּית דָּוִד, "house of David." *See also* construct chain; construct state.

absolutive. *adj.* Generally any *nominal that has no *affixes. *See also* ergative.

absorption. *n.* The power of one syntactical element to "absorb" the force or meaning of another. This is characteristic of the *inseparable preposition בְּ. (e.g., the *conjunction כַּאֲשֶׁר, "like, as, according to, when").

abstract/abstract noun. *n.* A noun that describes something that is nonconcrete or existential, such as love, strength or truth. Also referred to as nonanimates, these are to be contrasted with concrete nouns such as man, pot or trees. *See also* animate; inanimate.

Abyssinian. *See* Geʿez.

accent. *n.* In general linguistics, the syllable that receives the greatest *stress in pronunciation. BH employs a complex array of accent signs with even qualitative and tonal differences. The uses of BH accents are: (1) mark the *tone syllable; (2) punctuation indicators; and (3) *cantillation marks that act as musical signs for chanting the text in synagogue worship. Within BH there are also two classes of accent: *disjunctive (separating) and *conjunctive (joining) accents. BH has secondary accents besides the primary accent. Joüon §15; MNK §9; GKC §15. *See also* prepositive; postpositive; impositive.

accented syllable. *See* tone syllable.

accentuation, upper and lower. *n.* The accentuation points in the MT that appear above (supralinear) and below (sublinear) the consonantal text. *See also* accent.

acceptation. *n.* Within the field of *lexicography, the general publicly accepted meaning of a word. *See also* denotation.

accidence. *n.* The "accidental" attributes of an entity, to be distinguished from substance or essence in a theoretical linguistic framework. For example, one may say that the essence of a bicycle is that it has two wheels, handlebars, a seat and pedals, while its size and color are "accidental." Likewise, accidence in grammar generally refers to inflection. By changing *affixes, one modifies word meaning. Therefore, traditional grammarians would speak of words having the same substance while differing in accidence. *See also* inflection; morphology.

accidental perfective. *See* prophetic perfect.

accretion. *n.* In *textual criticism, a form of accidental or purposeful additions to a manuscript over time.

accusative. *n.* The noun case of the *direct object. The direct object is the recipient of the verbal action committed by the subject (e.g., "He hit *the ball*"). *See also* direct object marker. Joüon §125; GKC §117.

accusative ending. *See* locative *he*.

accusative of limitation. *n.* An *appositive in which the *adjective limits a noun by simple *juxtaposition.

accusative particle. *See* direct object marker.

acoustic phonetics. *See* phonetics.

acronym. *n.* The employment of the first letters of a string of words to refer to all the words. It was often used as a mnemonic device among ancient Hebrew grammarians. For example, *begadkepat* is an acronym composed of the first letters of the names of the six *tenue consonants.

acrophony. *n.* The theory that alphabetic letter sounds were originally taken from names of objects that began with that sound. For example, the Northwest Semitic letter *bet* (BH בּ) is believed to be taken from the *Proto-Semitic word for "house" (BH בַּיִת).

acrostic. *n.* A structuring technique found in BH poetry that begins a new *strophe or *pericope with the consecutive letters of the alphabet (e.g., Ps 9—10; 119; Lam 1—4; Prov 31:10-31).

actants. *n.* Sentence *nominals that represent the participants in the verbal action (i.e., the subject, object or indirect object of the verb).

action noun. *n.* A noun that labels an action or process (e.g., communication).

active-passive sequence. *n.* A form of BH literary *parallelism in which an *active verb is followed by its *cognate *passive in the following *strophe (e.g., Qal followed by Niphal); also called a factitive-passive sequence.

active verb. *See* active voice.

active voice. *n.* The verbal classification in which the subject commits the action of the verb (e.g., "John *pets* the dog"). *See also* passive voice.

ad sensum. Lat. "according to sense." An utterance translated according to contextual meaning rather than strict grammatical *concord.

adaptation. *n.* The conforming of *loanwords to the phonetic patterns of another language.

adjacency pair. *n.* Two utterances in which the second is a requisite or typical answer to the first (e.g., "How are you?" and "I am fine").

adjectival. *adj.* A broad linguistic classification that describes anything, from a word to an entire clause, that modifies a noun; also referred to as *adnominal. *See also* adverbial; nominal; verbal.

adjectival attribute. *See* attributive adjective.

adjectival phrase. *n.* A word group (lacking predication) that acts in the same capacity as an adjective, namely, to modify a noun. In "The child with red hair is playing alone," the prepositional phrase "with red hair" functions adjectivally.

adjectival predicate. *See* predicate adjective.

adjective. *n.* A word employed to describe, limit or qualify a noun. It gives further clarity to the noun being modified. BH is known for its shortage of genuine adjectives and subsequently relies heavily on the *construct state for the modification of nouns. *See also* attributive adjective; adjectival phrase; predicate adjective.

adjunct/adjunctive. *n.* or *adj.* (1) A sentence element that is unnecessary and thus an *omissible or *optional constituent. In "He built a home for her," the adjunctive "for her" is grammatically unnecessary to the sentence (contrast with *objective accusative or *complement). (2) In BH *adjunct* may also refer to a *waw conjunction understood with the force of "also." *See also* adverbial accusative.

adjunction. *n.* Any addition of an *omissible element to modify a necessary element.

adnominal. *adj.* A broad linguistic classification that describes anything that is "added to" a noun. Adnominals such as *adjectives or *prepositional phrases in some way modify a noun. *See also* adverbial.

adnomination n. A wordplay in which the meaning and the phonetic value of the words are similar or alike. *See also* onomatopoeia.

adposition. *n.* A general term for all *prepositions and postpositions.

adverb. *n.* Words or particles that modify or clarify the meaning of a verb as well as other adverbials and adjectivals (e.g., "The turtle moved [verb] slowly [adverb]"). Joüon §102; MNK §11.6; GKC §100. *See also* adjective.

adverbial. *adj.* A broad linguistic classification for anything that modifies a verb, including *adverbs, *adverbial phrases and the like.

adverbial clause. *See* nominal clause.

adverbial accusative. *adj.* In classical grammar, the employment of any noun or adjective adverbially; Hebrew and Semitic linguists now tend to favor the term "adverbial adjunct" or simply "adjunct" for such constructions, since they do not really function as *complements. MNK §33.1; *IBHS* §10.1-2.

adverbial apposition. *See* accusative of limitation.

adverbial element. *n.* A broad classification of any sentential element (word, *particle, *syntagm, *phrase or *clause) that modifies a verb.

adverbial predicate. *n.* In classical grammar, the expression of predication with a copular verb plus a prepositional phrase, such as "The man is [copular verb] in the house [prep. phrase]." BH does not possess an exact equivalent to English *copulatives, though the *existential particles and the so-called *pronominal copula are closely related.

adversative clause. *n.* A clause that expresses an adverse or contradictory circumstance. In English it is indicated by the coordinating conjunction "but." In BH it is usually conveyed by a *conjunctive *waw* (וְ), less commonly by כִּי אִם and sometimes simply by כִּי. It may also be implied by the *juxtaposition of clauses (e.g., Gen 17:5: וְלֹא־יִקָּרֵא עוֹד אֶת־שִׁמְךָ אַבְרָם וְהָיָה שִׁמְךָ אַבְרָהָם, "No longer shall your name be called Abram, *but your name shall be Abraham*"). Joüon §172; GKC §163.

aetiology. See *etiology*.

affected. *n.* Any noun that receives the action of the verb and existed prior to it. In an *active *transitive clause, the affected is the *direct object of the verb (e.g., "The car struck *the pole*"). In a passive clause, the subject is the affected (e.g., "*The pole* was struck by the car"). *See also* effected.

affected object. *See* direct object.

affirmative adverb. *n.* An adverb that is used to imply surety or certainty to the verbal action, such as *surely, truly* and *indeed*.

affix. *n.* A generic term for a *bound morpheme, including all *prefixes, *infixes and *suffixes.

afformative. *n./adj.* A general term comprising all *prefixes, *infixes and *suffixes.

affricate. *n.* A *phoneme that combines the properties of a *fricative and a *plosive, that is, the full momentary restriction of the airflow and burst (plosive) as well as the tightened air passage (fricative). In BH and BA, the צ is an example of an affricate. It is also called an assibilate.

Afroasiatic. *adj.* Pertaining to languages formerly referred to by the outdated nomenclature Hamito-Semitic and spoken in Asia and North Africa. The Asiatic side consists of the Semitic languages; the North African branch includes languages such as Afrasian, Lisramic, Berber, Coptic and its extinct counterpart, ancient *Egyptian.

agent. *n.* The noun committing the verbal action in a clause. The agent may theoretically be the subject of an active verb or the indirect object of a *passive verb. Some use it narrowly for just the noun committing the action of the passive verb.

agentive. *adj.* Pertaining to the verbal *agent.

agentless. *adj.* The lack of a verbal agent in a clause.

agglutinative language. *n.* A language that combines long strings of *morphemes into a single word unit. A complete sentence may even be expressed by one word. BH and BA both possess a prominence of agglutinative properties (e.g., יִשְׁמָרְךָ, "He shall keep you"). *See also* polysynthetic language; isolating language; inflectional language.

aggregate. *See* collective noun.

agreement. *See* concord.

Akkadian. *n.* One of the major language groupings of the ancient Near East. The name is derived from the ancient city of Akkad, and as a language family it originated in the Sumer and Akkad locale of Mesopotamia. It is broken into two subdialects: Babylonian and Assyrian. As a Semitic language, it shares a relative vocabulary and other linguistic properties with languages such as BH and Arabic. It was epigraphically represented with the *syllabic cuneiform writing system, which it borrowed from the more ancient *Sumerian.

Aktionsart. *n.* A term for verbal *aspect that is *kind* of action in contrast to *tense* or *time* of action. It and its related term *Aspekt* emphasize how an action is committed, not when. *Aktionsart* is concerned with concepts such as completion, *causation, *durativity and *iterativity in verbal action. *See also* aspect. *IBHS* §20.2

aleph prostheticum. *See* prosthetic *aleph*.

Aleppo Codex. *n.* A Hebrew manuscript dating to approximately A.D. 930 and attributed to Shelomo ben Buya'a. It is an important textual witness to the Aaron *ben Asher pointing tradition.

allative. *See* locative.

allegory. *n.* An extended metaphor or a fictional story meant to convey truths other than what the surface story is about. Writers of allegories often use animals or inanimate objects as characters, thus forcing the reader to search for a deeper meaning. There is really no allegory in the Hebrew Bible, with the possible exception of the invective parable of Jotham in Judges 9:7-15. The New Testament does, however, offer a fine example in Galatians 4:21-31.

alliteration. *n.* The repetition of consonantal sounds at the beginning of a word; this is observed in Hebrew poetry.

allography. Gk. "other writing." —*n.* The use of a *logogram or *ideogram as a substitute for terminology in one's own language.

allomorph. *n.* A variant form of a *morpheme. In such cases, the unit has the same meaning but may take a different form based on context. For example, in BA the forms הָ and יהִ are both third masculine singular pronominal suffixes, and הִמֹּו, הִמֹּון and אִנּוּן are all forms of the third masculine plural independent personal pronoun. Allomorphism may also be understood phonologically, such as in *aspiration or *allophones caused by phonological *positional variation.

allophone. *n.* A sound that can be classified among a certain category or pair of sounds but is distinguishable in practice. For example, there is a distinguishable pronunciation difference between *p* at the beginning of a word and at the end. At the beginning it is *aspirated (a quick puff of air may be detected in pronunciation by placing the forefinger before the lips); at the end of a word, it is *unaspirated (there is no detectable puff when pronounced correctly) and functions as a *stop. Allophones are most often caused by their placement within a word and in relation to other letters, so they are also referred to as *positional variants.

allusion. *n.* An indirect statement for referring to something usually held in common by the speaker/author and hearer/reader. Biblical writers of both Testaments commonly use words and phrases to bring to mind other key biblical texts that illuminate their message.

alphabet. *n.* Alphabetic writing seems to have originated in Egypt under the influence of hieroglyphics. The concept was taken and refined by the Phoenicians, who spread it throughout the Mediterranean world; in time it became the basis for all alphabets. The alphabet employed in the MT is actually an Aramaic script often referred to as the square character script and is composed of twenty-two consonants. The basic order of letters in the Semitic alphabet is very ancient, and an alphabetic writing system has been attested at Wadi el-Hol in Egypt as early as the nineteenth century B.C. Joüon §5; MNK §4; GKC §§5-6.

alphabetic poems. *See* acrostic.

alveolar. *See* dentals.

ambiguity. *n.* The common problem of how language expressions fail to convey sharply the intended meaning or leave open the possibility of multiple interpretations. Linguists recognize both deliberate *ambiguity and unintended ambiguity, a result of the limitations of language. Linguists further distinguish between two formal types of ambiguity: grammatical ambiguity results when the words in an utterance are not clear by reason of grammar or syntax; lexical ambiguity arises in contexts where words have multiple meanings, leaving more than one meaning possible.

Amharic. *See* Ethiopic.

Ammonite. *n.* The language spoken by the ancient people of Ammon, a neighboring ethnic group of Israel. Ammonite is a Northwest Semitic dialect within the Canaanite subfamily and shows affinity with ancient Hebrew.

Amoraim. Mishnaic Hebrew "speakers, expounders." —*n.* Rabbinic teachers residing in Palestine and Babylon between the third and sixth centuries A.D. who were responsible for the *talmudic writings and *haggadic *midrashim.

Amorite. *n.* A Semitic language attested in *Akkadian documents from Babylon, Mari and other sites in Syria-Palestine starting in about the beginning of the second millennium B.C.

anachronism. *n.* A reference to something in terms that developed later, such as an element in an ancient manuscript (e.g., a *toponym or *patronym) that is situated in a historical context that predates its usage. Many critical scholars cite the references to Philistines in Genesis 21:32, 34; 26:1, 8, 14-15, 18 as anachronisms because most available archaeological evidence for the migration of the Sea Peoples is no sooner than the Late Bronze Age.

anacoluthon. *n.* The act of breaking a thought in mid-sentence for another sentence structure. It often indicates an author losing his or her train of thought, but it may also represent a purposeful idiom of expression (e.g., Gen 23:13: אַךְ אִם־אַתָּה לוּ שְׁמָעֵנִי נָתַתִּי כֶּסֶף הַשָּׂדֶה קַח מִמֶּנִּי וְאֶקְבְּרָה אֶת־מֵתִי שָׁמָּה, "If you—please hear me, I will give silver for the field—take it from me and I will bury my dead there!"). GKC §167.2.

anacrusis. *n.* A construction in which one or more unaccented syllables at the beginning of a verse stands outside the regular pattern and is thus reliant upon another accented syllable. The term is used in reference to BH poetry but also assumes the presence of *meter, which is debated.

anadiplosis. *n.* The reduplication of a word or phrase in the second *colon of poetic verse. This form of repetition carries a theme from one colon to the next to establish a progression in thought (e.g., Ps 1:2: "But his delight is *in the law of the LORD,* / *and in his law* he meditates day and night").

anaphora. *n.* (1) Words that "point back" to another word; to be contrasted with *cataphora, which point forward to a referent. Pronouns of all types are considered to be anaphoric signs. Personal pronouns especially fit this category in that they point back to an antecedent noun. *Resumptive pronouns (occasional in BH and common in BA) resume the idea of the antecedent without restating it. (2) The term is also used in the study of poetry to refer to the linking of verses into bicola, tricola, and so forth by employing the same word or phrase at the beginning of each line (also called *anadiplosis).

anaphoric. *adj.* Pertaining to any sentential element that points back to a previous *referent. *See also* anaphora; cataphoric

anaptyxis. *n.* The development of an extra vowel to smooth awkward pronunciation, such as in the common pronunciation of the English word *athlete* by inserting an *e* vowel sound between the *th* and the *l*, making it ath-e-lete. In BH many scholars point to the second *segol in *segholate nouns as a prime example though this is contested. Anaptyxis is attested in most Semitic dialects. *See also* prosthesis.

anarthrous. *adj.* A word that has no definite article or generally any word that is indefinite. *See also* articular; definite; indefinite.

anastrophe. *n.* The purposeful modification of normative *word order for stylistic reasons or for the sake of emphasis. *See also* free inversion.

Anatolian. *n.* A subbranch of the *Indo-European languages that includes *Hittite among its membership.

animate. *adj.* Entities that are living things (e.g., a lion, person or people) as opposed to static, material objects (*inanimates; e.g., a rock) or theoretical concepts, ideas and emotions (*nonanimates or *abstracts; e.g., love).

animate pronoun. *n.* A pronoun that has an *interrogative meaning "who?" and is classified under the larger idea of indefinites. The BH animate pronoun is מִי, and the common Semitic animate particle is *man*, which is also attested in BH (Ex 16:15). Animate pronouns are commonly used in both direct and rhetorical questions (e.g., Ex 3:11 "Who am I that I should go to Pharaoh?"). They are also employed in a *relative sense. Joüon §§37, 144; MNK §43.3; GKC §37; IBHS §18.2-3. *See also* inanimate pronoun; indefinite.

annexion, annexation. *See* construct state.

anomaly. *n.* A contradiction to standard rules. When a *morpheme or *grapheme displays anomalous usage, it is usually an error, though in some cases, such as poetic contexts, it may be purposeful.

antagonist. *n.* The character who is set against the *protagonist in any *narrative.

antanaclasis. *n.* The repetition of a *lexeme (word) with a divergent or even an antithetical sense.

antecedent. *n.* The co-referent that any pronoun points back to. For example, in "Jimmy was running in the hall and tripped over his shoelace," the antecedent of the pronoun *his* is *Jimmy*.

antepenult. *n.* The third syllable from the end in a word with three or more syllables. When an accent is placed on this syllable it is commonly described as "antepenultimate."

antepenultima. *See* antepenult.

anterior. *adj.* When used with reference to *phonemes, it describes their articulation toward the frontal part of the mouth.

anterior construction. *n.* A *clause that expresses events or a state of being that took place or existed prior to the main narrated sequence of events. Such a construction usually provides background material for the main narration. In BH it is often marked by the use of a fronted subject and a verbal transition (from *wayyiqtol* to *qatal*), such as in Genesis 3:1: וְהַנָּחָשׁ הָיָה עָרוּם מִכֹּל חַיַּת הַשָּׂדֶה אֲשֶׁר עָשָׂה יְהוָה אֱלֹהִים וַיֹּאמֶר אֶל־הָאִשָּׁה, "Now the serpent was more crafty than any creature of the field which YHWH Elohim had created. And he said unto the woman . . ."

anticipatory assimilation. *n.* *See* regressive assimilation.

anthropomorphism. *n.* The ascription of human characteristics to God.

anthropopathism. *n.* The ascription of humanlike emotions to God.

anticipative pronoun. *See* cataphora.

antilogomena. *n.* Books of the biblical *canon whose authenticity has been questioned in church history.

antimeria. *n.* A subclassification of *metonymy; the artistic use of a descriptive term for a closely associated noun. In "The white fell gently upon the Canadian forest," the adjective *white* is employed as a *substantive to refer to snow. In BH, antimeria is commonly found in poetry but is not limited to it.

antiphon. *n.* Poetic verse that is responsively read in conjunction with the singing of a liturgy.

antiphrasis. *n.* The use of a word in a sense opposite to its normal meaning, often for the sake of irony or rhetorical effect. *See also* litotes.

antistrophe. *n.* A form of *parallelism in which there is *repetition of a word or phrase at the end of two or more *strophes.

antithesis. *n.* A contrast of some sort, such as between word pairs, such as *good* and *bad*, or between clauses or strophes, as in *antithetic parallelism.

antithetic conjunction. *n.* A conjunction that indicates constrast, such as *but* or *unless. See also* adversative clause.

antithetic parallelism. *n.* A parallel *bicolon structure in which the second line contrasts the first. That is, the A colon makes a statement, and the B colon declares its corresponding opposite. *See also* parallelism; synonymous parallelism; synthetic parallelism.

antithetic sentence. *n.* A compound sentence in which the two main clauses possess antithetic relationship to one another. *See also* conjunctive sentence; contrastive sentence; chiastic sentence.

antonym. *n.* A word that stands as a relative opposite to another word. Antonyms are further broken down into classes of *graded and non-graded. *See also* synonym.

aphaeresis. *n.* The dropping of the initial vowel or consonant during inflection. It is most common in BH when a weak letter (א, י, ל, נ) is not supported by a full vowel, such as the verb meaning "to take" inflected in the Qal imperative: a hypothetical לְקַח appears as קַח (e.g., Gen 19:15). Joüon §17d. *See also* apocope; syncope.

Aphel. *n.* The Aramaic *causative stem that is marked in most forms by an *aleph* preformative.

aphesis. *n.* The dropping of a *word-initial *unstressed vowel. *See also* aphaeresis.

aphorism. *n.* A terse summary statement that is meant to express a wise observation or general principle of life. *See* apothegm.

apocalypse. *n.* Generally defined as a *genre of Old Testament, intertestamental and New Testament period writing characterized by the use of ecstatic prophetic oracles, vivid imagery of a final judgment and elaborate symbolism. The books of Joel and Daniel are known for their use of apocalyptic imagery. Some scholars define it more narrowly as a interpretation of history in allegorical images, in contrast to eschatology, which is the ecstatic oracular vision of future events, especially the end of the age.

apocope, apocopation. *n.* The loss of a vowel quality or silent letter at the end of a word, usually due to lack of *accentuation. In BH it is most common with final-ה verbs and the *jussive mood, in which apocopation is used as a jussive mood marker, though it also occurs in nouns. Joüon §17f; GKC §48. *See also* aphaeresis; syncope.

Apocrypha. *n.* A collection of intertestamental Jewish literature that is not included in the Jewish and Christian canons but is classified as "deuterocanonical" in the Roman Catholic tradition.

apodictic law. *n.* A term introduced by Albrecht Alt to refer to a form of legal writing that makes absolute demands upon the recipient ("You shall not. . .") and is to be contrasted with *casuistic law. The *Decalogue is classified as apodictic law.

apodosis. *n.* The main clause of a *conditional sentence that is preceded by the dependent *conditional clause (*protasis.) In BH the apodosis is usually marked by a *waw of apodosis (translated "then"). Joüon §176; GKC §158.

apophony. *n.* (1) In *synchronic linguistics, a vowel alternation in the process of *morphology. (2) In *diachronic linguistics, a permanent vowel change or *gradation made over time in linguistic evolution. *See* sound shift.

apophthegm. *See* apothegm.

aposiopesis. *n.* A communicative pause or momentary silence in articulation, often to provide a dramatic effect, or the dropping or concealment of an entire sentence that is necessary for completion of the thought. This is often found in contexts in which the omitted sentence would describe either horrible or offensive circumstances. GKC §167.1.

apostrophe. *n.* The literary technique of speaking to an absent person or entity as if present. In BH it is most common in poetry and prophetic oracles (e.g., Jer 47:6 NASB: "Ah, sword of the LORD, How long will you not be quiet? Withdraw into your sheath; Be at rest and stay still").

apothegm. *n.* A brief saying or statement consisting of an important truth, principle or maxim. This term is widely used but variously defined in *form criticism.

appellation. *n.* The use of inherently descriptive nomenclature, such as a name that describes what is actually being referred to (e.g., הָעַי, "the ruin"; הַלְּבָנוֹן, "the white [mountain]").

appellative. *adj.* Pertaining to *appellation.

apposition. *n.* (1) The placing of nouns in *juxtaposition (the same grammatical position, i.e., subject or object) to let one clarify the other. This may occur on both the word (*nominal apposition) and clause levels (*clausal apposition). In cases of BH nominal apposition, both nouns must agree in definiteness (e.g., 2 Sam 3:31: וְהַמֶּלֶךְ דָּוִד הֹלֵךְ אַחֲרֵי הַמִּטָּה, "*And the king, David,* followed after the casket"). (2) On the clause level, apposition is a form of literary *parallelism and is characteristic of BH poetry or lofty prose. Joüon §§131, 138; MNK §29; GKC §131; *IBHS* §12.

appositive. *n.* A word in *apposition.

Aquila. *n.* A Greek translation of the Hebrew Bible dating to about A.D. 130 and generally attributed to a disciple of Rabbi Akiba by the name of Aquila. It was produced in response to the Jewish community's rejection of the *Septuagint.

Arabic. *n.* A *South Semitic language attested in inscriptions as early as the fifth century B.C. and spread by the Islamic expansions of the fifth to seventh centuries A.D. Today it boasts a large variety of dialects. Classical Arabic is the language of the *Qur'an.

Aramaic. *n.* אֲרָמִית. A Northwest Semitic language that became the *lingua franca* of the ancient Near East from the period of Assyrian dominance until after Alexander's conquests, later to be replaced by Greek. It was originally spoken by the Aramean tribes and was adopted as the official language of the Persian Empire (Imperial Aramaic; German *Reichsaramaisch*). It is closely related to BH, and short portions of the Old Testament are composed in Aramaic (two words in Gen 31:47; Ezra 4:8—6:18; 7:12-26; Dan 2:4b—7:28; Jer. 10:11, besides numerous Aramaisms). It became the native tongue of Palestine throughout the *intertestamental and New Testament periods. Aramaic is categorized into two major subdialects: West Aramaic, including Nabatean, Palmyrene, Jewish Palestinian Aramaic, Samaritan Aramaic and Christian Palestinian Aramaic; and East Aramaic, including Babylonian Aramaic, Mandean and Syriac.

Aramaism. *n.* The random occurrence of an *Aramaic word in a *manuscript, such as the word בַר, "son," in Psalm 2:12.

archaism. *n.* The presence of archaic terms in more recent manuscripts. A distinction is often made between archaism and archaizing, the former for ancient terms remaining in an edited text, and the latter for the purposeful placement of ancient terms into newer texts to make them sound older or more authoritative. *See also* modernizing; anachronism; smoothing.

archaizing. *See* archaism.

archetypes. *n.* Fundamental elements that may be found in almost every narration, such as character types, plot motifs and literary images.

aretalogy. *n.* Used variously in *literary criticism, a compilation of stories of virtuous characters within a biographical genre that expresses the virtue of the main character.

arthrous. *See* articular.

article. *n.* A grammatical element that indicates definiteness or indefiniteness. English has both *definite (the) and *indefinite (a, an) articles. BH has only the definite article הַ plus the doubling of the initial consonant of the word to which it is *prefixed. Indefiniteness is expressed simply by the lack of the article and context. Joüon §35; MNK §24.4; GKC §35. *See also* anarthrous.

articular. *adj.* Having a definite *article. The term is loosely used with reference to proper nouns. Joüon §35; MNK §24.4; GKC §35. *See also* definite; indefinite; anarthrous.

articulatory phonetics. *See* phonetics.

acensive. *adj.* Pertaining to the peak or climax of a narrative.

Ashkenazim. *n.* Jews, particularly the rabbinic scholars, who settled in Northern Europe (especially Germany) during the medieval period.

Ashkenazic. *adj.* Referring to a tradition of Hebrew pronunciation that developed among the Jews of northern Europe, mainly in Germany. It takes its name from the *Ashkenazim who were the rabbinic scholars of northern Europe. *See also* Sephardic.

aspect. *n.* A verbal categorization that focuses upon kind of action rather than time of action (i.e., *tense). The English term *aspect* is used in reference to two different German grammatical terms: *Aspekt* and *Aktionsart*. Both refer to kind of action; however, *Aspekt* connotes the nuances of progressiveness and perfectivity and defines the action in relation to its completion (e.g., "I am leaving" or "I had left"). *Aktionsart* connotes such concepts as *voice (*active, *reflexive and *passive) as well as *transitivity and *intransitivity. Since the nuances of these terms are so subtle and are both referred to by English *aspect*, some caution is in order when interacting with the linguistic literature. Some linguists use the terms interchangeably, while others do not.

Aspekt. *See* aspect.

aspirantization. *See* spirantization.

aspiration, aspirate. *See* spirantization.

asseveration. *n./v.* The use of a word or word *collocation to convey emphasis or strong affirmation. This may come in the form of a self-imprecation (curse) or exhortation, such as חָלִילָה לִי, "Far be it from me," or אִם־לֹא, "certainly not!" In the Hebrew Bible, these are characteristic of covenant and oath-type contexts (e.g., Ruth 1:17).

asseverative. *adj.* Pertaining to any utterance conveying strong affirmation. *See* asseveration.

asseverative clause. *n.* A sentence or clause that conveys strong affirmation and commitment, often in BH in oath contexts. Joüon §§164-165; GKC §149. *See* asseverative.

assibilate. *n.* A subclassification of *affricates that is composed of a *stop followed by a *sibilant *fricative.

assimilation. *n.* The combining of two differing sounds into one, most often occurring for the purpose of smoothing pronunciation (e.g., in + mediate = immediate). There are two kinds of assimilation in BH: *progressive and *regressive. Assimilation is common in initial-*nun* verbs (e.g., נפל in the *imperfect becomes יִפֹּל, not יִנְפֹּל). It is commonly found when a *reflexive stem (*Hithpael) is

used with a *word-initial *dental letter (e.g., the participle מִתְדַּבֵּר
becomes מִדַּבֵּר). Jöuon §17g.

assonance. *n.* A similarity of sounds between syllables or words.
Authors often use rhyme or similarity of sound in the accented
vowels for the purpose of aesthetic appeal as well as unity, mem-
orability and, occasionally, emphasis.

Assyrian. *n.* A Semitic language and subdialect of *Akkadian that
was the official language of the Assyrian Empire and was epigraphically represented on stone or clay using a *syllabic *cuneiform script.

Assyrian character script. *See* square character script.

asyndeton. *n.* (1) The relating of *clauses and *strophes by juxtaposition (i.e., the dropping of *prepositions and *conjunctions linking coordinate relationships) when clarity of context allows it. This
is most often found in BH poetry. On the clause level, it refers specifically to the dropping of a *waw*-conjunctive. (2) Used negatively,
a reference to poor syntax. Jöuon §177. *See also* syndeton.

asyndetic. *adj.* Pertaining to coordination without coordinating particles or conjunctives.

athe merachiq, otheh merachoq. (Mishnaic Hebrew אָתֵי מֵרַחִיק; Aramaic אוֹתֶה מֵרָחוֹק) A term coined by early Hebrew grammarians
to describe the hardening of the initial consonant of an accented
first syllable or accented *monosyllabic word by use of a conjunctive, *euphonic *dagesh forte*. This usually occurs when the preceding word is accented *milel* (*penultima) and ends with a vowel
sound such as ה‍ָ or ה‍ֶ. For example, הוֹשִׁיעָה נָּא in Psalm 118:25 is
pronounced ho-shi-an-na, not ho-shi-ah-na. The accent on שִׁ
causes the *nun* in נָא to be doubled. See also שָׁבִיתָ שֶּׁבִי in Psalm
65:18 (MT 19), which is pronounced sha-bi-tash-she-bi, not sha-bi-
ta-she-bi. GKC §20f-g; Jöuon §18j. *See also* dechiq.

atnach. *n.* A strong *disjunctive *pause marking the mid-point of a
verse in the MT (ˌ).

attenuation. *n.* A vowel reduction that may result in a full vowel being reduced to a *vocal *shewa* or any reduction of a *strong-vowel
quality to a weaker-vowel quality.

attributive. *adj.* Pertaining to attribution or modification of a sentence element.

attributive adjective. *n.* Any word that subscribes attributes to another word. In BH, it usually follows the noun being modified and always agrees with it in gender, number and definiteness (e.g., Gen 8:20: הַבְּהֵמָה הַטְּהוֹרָה, "clean beasts"). GKC §132. *See also* adjective; predicate adjective.

attributive genitive. *n.* A genitive that conveys attribution.

audible *shewa*. *See* vocal *shewa*.

auditory. *adj.* Pertaining to the faculty of hearing.

auditory phonetics. *See* phonetics.

aural. *adj.* Another term used for "oral" communication or spoken language, but carrying with it an emphasis on the listening aspects of verbal communication.

auxiliary verb. *n.* In English grammar, a narrow class of adverbials used to further indicate and clarify the time (*tense) of a verb; also called a "helping verb." The simple sentence, "He comes," gives the idea of a present, continuous action, but with the auxiliary *will*, it indicates future tense (e.g., "He *will* come"). Other examples are *had, has, had been, has been* and the like. As auxiliaries, they cannot stand alone but are supportive (*adverbial) in function.

ayin-**guttural.** *n.* A BH weak verb with a *guttural letter in the *word-medial position of the *triliteral *root (e.g., the verb פַּעַל, "to do or make"). They are also called II-guttural verbs. Joüon §69; MNK §18.2; GKC §64.

ayin-*waw*, *ayin*-*yod*. *n.* A weak verb with either a ו or י in the medial position of the *triliteral *root (e.g., the verb לִין or לוּן, "to lodge" or "stay over"). They are also called II-*waw* or II-*yod* verbs. Joüon §§80-81; MNK §18.8; GKC §72.

B

Babylonian. *n.* A dialect of *Akkadian that was indigenous to the people and geographical region of ancient Babylon. It was epigraphically represented on stone and clay in *syllabic *cuneiform script.

back vowel. *n.* Any *vowel that is pronounced toward the rear of the mouth, such as long *u*, short *u*, long *o*, short *o* and *ah*. In BH these sounds are represented by *shureq, *qibbuts, *holem, *holem waw* and *qamets. *See also* front vowel; rounded vowel.

back-clipping. *See* apocope.

back-referencing. *n.* (1) Reference back to a previous sentence, often because the latter is contingent on the former (e.g., "Having done A, John did B"). (2) In a literary sense, the linking of ideas and events over larger portions of text.

ballast. *n.* Any element of syntax or prepositions that are used to "stabilize" or more sharply define meaning.

ballast preposition. *n.* Any preposition used to reinforce the meaning of an utterance or for clarification.

base. *n.* Theoretically, any form to which morphological processes may be applied, but more specifically a verbal stem or root word in the Semitic languages. *See also* root.

base stem. *See* B-stem; Qal stem.

base vowel. *See* characteristic vowel.

begadkepat. *n.* An *acronym for the six Hebrew letters that take a *dagesh lene* (ב, ג, ד, כ, פ, ת) and undergo a softening in pronunciation when the *dagesh* is dropped (*aspiration). Over time the changes in pronunciation have been lost in four out of the six letters, only ב and פ still exhibiting aspiration. They may also take a *dagesh forte* (signifying a doubling), but close attention to the rules of *syllable structure helps distinguish between them. Joüon §§50, 19; MNK §4.2; GKC §21. *See also* dagesh; mappiq.

beheading. *n.* The dropping of the *head noun in a genitival relationship. This is often done in *colloquial speech for simplification and shortening. In BH this may be observed by comparing Genesis 15:18, where the Euphrates River is referred to as נְהַר־פְּרָת, "River of Euphrates," and Genesis 2:14, where the same construction is beheaded as just פְּרָת, "Euphrates."

ben Asher. *n.* A medieval Tiberian recension of the Hebrew text attributed to the ben Asher family. The ben Asher family was responsible for producing *Codex Cairensis, the *Allepo Codex and *Codex Leningradensis, which are the basis for modern editions of the MT.

ben Naphtali. *n.* A medieval Tiberian recension of the Hebrew text attributed to ben Naphtali.

benediction. *n.* Any formal pronouncement of blessing toward or for the sake of another person or entity.

benefactive. *adj.* Pertaining to any clausal construction (usually *reflexive) in which the subject acts toward the benefit of itself or out of its own self-interest. *See also* reflexive.

bestowal. *n.* The act of granting a privilege, property or gift to another entity. It is often found in BH with a causative stem and the so-called *double accusative.

beth. *n.* The second letter of BH, BA and Semitic alphabets in general (בּ). In BH it is employed as an *inseparable preposition, which is liberally used to convey a plethora of syntactical relationships.

beth causa. *n.* The use of the *beth* preposition with a causative nuance.

beth comitantiae. *n.* The use of the *beth* preposition to indicate accompaniment, such as "with" or "also." It is used to indicate other entities accompanying the subject in committing the verbal action.

beth essentiae. *n.* The use of the *beth* preposition with the idea of *as* (e.g., Ex 6:3: בְּאֵל שַׁדָּי, "*as* El Shaddai").

beth instrumenti. *n.* The instrumental use of the *beth* preposition to indicate "by," "through" or "by what means" an action was committed.

beth locale. *n.* The locative use of the *beth* preposition (e.g., "to," "toward," "at").

beth pretii. *n.* The use of the *beth* preposition to convey a cost or consequence for which the verbal action was committed.

BHS. *n.* *Biblia Hebraica Stuttgartensia.*

bicolon. *n.* A verse structure of poetry having two *cola (lines) that are related thematically and rhythmically. *pl.* bicola. *See also* colon.

biconsonantal root. *See* biliteral root.

bilabial. *n.* A letter pronounced by the touching of both lips, such as מ (*m*) or ב (*b*).

bilabial plosive. *n.* A letter pronounced by the touching of both lips followed by an outward burst, as in the pronunciation of בּ and פּ when represented with the hardening dot. *See also* plosive; labiodentals; fricative; continuant.

bilingualism. *n.* (1) The use of two languages by a person who is semi- or fully fluent in both. (2) In a theoretical linguistic framework, how languages that are used together in close geographical proximity cause *interference with each other, which results in the use of *loanwords and general *borrowing.

biliteral root. *n.* A verbal root composed of two *root consonants, which in BH constitutes a *monosyllabic word; also referred to as a diconsonantal or biconsonantal root. Most of those in BH became biliteral because of a *middle *waw* or *yod* dropping out in antiquity. These are commonly classified as *ayin-waw* or *ayin-yod* weak verbs. *See also* triliteral root; quadriliteral root.

binder. *See* copula.

binding. *adj.* In classical Greek grammar, pertaining to anything that binds sentence elements.

binominal. *adj.* Referring to the use of two nominals in parallel lines for one entity, such as in Ruth 4:11: "May you prosper in *Ephrathah* and gain renown in *Bethlehem.*"

binyan, binyanim. *See* verb stem.

bisyllabic. *adj.* Referring to a word consisting of two syllables.

block character script. *See* square character script.

borrowing. *n.* The sharing and eventual assimilation of words from one language to another, usually by reason of geographical *bilingualism. *See also* loanword.

bound morpheme. *n.* A *morpheme that cannot stand alone but must be attached to a *free morpheme in order to be used (e.g., BH *pronominal suffixes).

bound structure. *See* construct state.

broad *qamets*. *n.* A regular *qamets* as distinguished from the *qamets hatuph* (*narrow *qamets*). Broad *qamets* is an *a*-class *long vowel, while the narrow *qamets* is an *o*-class *short vowel. They can be distinguished only by attention to syllable structure and accent. *See also qamets hatuph.*

broken construct chain. *n.* The intervention of a grammatical element, such as a preposition or other suffixed particle, between the *construct noun and the *absolute noun.

B-stem, base stem. *n.* The most basic stem vowel construction, also known as the *G-stem (ground stem) in the other Semitic dialects and corresponding to BH Qal. It is the stem from which all other *derived stems are built.

C

caesura. *n.* A stop or *metrical division in a line of poetic verse. It may be contrasted with a *pause (a momentary rest between *cola) in that a caesura is the dividing point in the middle of a colon.

Cairensis, Codex. *n.* A *masoretic manuscript of the *Former Prophets and *Latter Prophets, believed to have been copied and
pointed by Moses *ben Asher and dated to circa 895 A.D.

calque. *See* loanword.

Canaanite dialects. *n.* A subclass of the Northwest Semitic languages that includes those dialects spoken in and around the
greater territory of Syria-Palestine, including *Classical Biblical
Hebrew, Late Biblical Hebrew, *Phoenician, *Ugaritic and some
lesser-attested dialects such as *Moabite and *Ammonite. The
Canaanite dialects are often distinguished by a particular vowel
change known as the *Canaanite shift.

Canaanite shift. *n.* A sound shift common to the Canaanite dialects
of the Northwest Semitic *phylum (e.g., BH, Phoenician) that re-
places an *a*-class vowel with an *o*-class vowel sound. This *sound
shift is observable in texts as early as the *Amarna letters. *See also*
systematic correspondence.

canon. *n.* (1) In general, anything by which all other things are
judged or evaluated. (2) Specifically, any compilation of authoritative literary works that provide the standard for a religious movement, especially the Hebrew Bible, Christian Bible or *Qur'an.

canonical. *adj.* Pertaining to membership among a canon.

canonical criticism. *n.* Primarily associated with Brevard S. Childs,
a form of *criticism that makes an accepted religious canon the
starting point of biblical interpretation. Although it is not an attempt to unify the various voices and traditions in the Bible, it
seeks to hear their corporate witness together, in contrast to traditional criticism, which focuses more on the disunity of the text or
canon and tends to be somewhat atomistic.

cantillation marks. *n.* The *hyperlinear and *sublinear system of
markings in the MT that guide the public reading of the Hebrew
Bible. The system of marking was devised by the *Amoraim and
analyzed by the *Masoretes. It acts as a sort of musical-tone representation system by which the text is chanted in public worship.
See also accent.

cardinal numerals. *n.* The regular counting numerals as employed
in mathematics (one, two, three, etc.). *See also* ordinal numeral.

case. *n.* The syntactic function of a noun or pronoun in a sentence.
Most linguists in the tradition of classical grammar take the view

that there are a total of four cases: nominative, genitive, dative and accusative. Others have posited as many as eight or more: *nominative (subject); *genitive (genus or possession; e.g., "of"); *ablative (separation; e.g., "from"); *dative (*indirect object); locative (location, position or relationship; e.g., "to, at"); *instrumental (means or instrumentality; e.g., "by, by means of"); *accusative (*direct object); and *vocative (direct address; also called a nominative of direct address). *See also* case marker; diptotic; triptotic.

case ending. *See* case marker.

case marker. *n.* In inflected languages, an inflectional form or *afformative added to a noun to indicate syntactic function in a sentence. It is important to distinguish between *case markers and actual *case function. While not all languages have case endings, all languages indicate case function in one way or another. There is evidence that early Hebrew probably had some case marking, but by the time of classical BH, it had fallen into disuse. BH came to indicate case function by a variety of methods, such as *juxtaposition, the *construct state, *word order, *prepositions and certain *particles and *deictic elements. Other Semitic languages (e.g., Ugaritic, Akkadian, Arabic) have retained some case marking.

casuistic law. *n.* A term introduced into the literary study of the Hebrew Bible and ancient Near Eastern legal documents by Albrecht Alt to refer to case law or a written precedent of how to rule in a particular scenario. Casuistic law is often marked by the use of conditional or temporal clauses ("If a man..." or "When a man..."), such as in Exodus 21:32. *See also* apodictic law.

casus instrumentalis. *See* instrumental.

casus pendens. *n.* A grammatical element that stands off from and is grammatically unrelated to the main sentence; also called a nominative absolute or a focus marker. It presents an object of focus, usually the subject, which is restated in the following sentence, such as, "*A great artist*, Picasso was a good illustrator," or אֵל אֱלֹהִים יְהוָה דִּבֶּר, "*God of gods*, YHWH spoke" (Ps 50:1a). Joüon §156; MNK §§34.5, 46.1; GKC §143.

catachresis. *n.* An incorrect use of language.

cataphora. *n.* A pronominal element that points forward to other words in a sentence or discourse; a pronoun or sentence element whose referent has not yet been stated but is anticipated; also called an anticipative pronoun (e.g., Ex 2:6: וַתִּרְאֵהוּ אֶת־הַיֶּלֶד, "and she saw *him*, the child").

cataphoric. *adj.* Descriptive of sentential elements that point forward to a coming nominal.

catena. *See* chain.

causal clause. *n.* A subordinate clause answering the question of how certain circumstances materialized or the cause of some state of being, such as in Amos 2:6: לֹא אֲשִׁיבֶנּוּ עַל־מִכְרָם בַּכֶּסֶף צַדִּיק, "I will not turn away the punishment thereof *because they sold the righteous for silver.*" Joüon §170; GKC §158.

causation construction. *n.* Any grammatical construction that expresses the concept of causation or one thing influencing another. *See also* causative stems.

causative. *adj.* Pertaining to any grammatical or syntactical indication of causation.

causative active. *See* Hiphil stem.

causative passive. *See* Hophal stem.

causative stems. *n.* Verbal vowel stems among the Semitic languages that indicate causation in the verb, such as the BH *Hiphil and *Hophal stems or the BA *Haphel, *Aphel and *Shaphel stems.

centripetal. *adj.* A term used synonymously with the *reflexive or *ingressive idea in BH verbal action (*Hithpael, *Niphal and other constructions). However, some grammarians make a fine distinction between the two, giving a nuance of isolation to "centripetal." *See also* reflexive.

chain. *n.* Any sequence of *free and *bound morphemes conveying meaning (e.g., a *syntagm).

chain-figure parallelism. *See* climactic parallelism.

Chaldee, Chaldean. *n.* A misnomer for the Aramaic found in Daniel and Ezra. This nomenclature arose because earlier Hebraists incorrectly deduced that the Aramaic in Ezra and Daniel was the native tongue of Babylon. *See also* Aramaic.

character types. *n.* The standard roles played in a narrative: e.g., protagonist, antagonist, hero, anti-hero and *femme fatale.*

characteristic vowel. *n.* The vowel quality located in the second vowel slot in a Hebrew root that often provides indication of verbal mode or aspect.

chiasmus. See chiastic sentence.

chiastic parallelism. *See* chiastic sentence.

chiastic sentence. *n.* A poetic literary structure, named after the Greek letter X, that forms an x pattern in strophic poetic verse. The pattern is often lost in translation but is quite noticeable in BH poetry, such as in Psalm 2:9:

> You *will break* them   **with a rod** of iron;
>
> X
>
> **like earthenware**   you *will shatter* them.

See also contrastive sentence; conjunctive sentence.

chrestomathy. *n.* A selection of literary excerpts compiled under one cover for instructional purposes.

circumlocution. *n.* (1) A rhetorically indirect or roundabout way of stating something; also called *periphrasis. For example, אַנְשֵׁי הַשֵּׁם, "men of the name" (Gen 6:4), implies renown or greatness. (2) In BH a grammatical reference to the use of a ל prep. to express an indefinite genitive rather than a definite genitive as the construct state (e.g., 1 Sam 16:18: בֵּן לְיִשַׁי, "a son of Jesse"; Ps 23:1: מִזְמוֹר לְדָוִד, "a psalm of David"). GKC §129.

circumstantial clause. *n.* A subordinate clause that clarifies the context or describes the attendant circumstances of the *main clause (e.g., Deut 5:23: וְהָהָר בֹּעֵר בָּאֵשׁ, "while the mountain was burning with fire"). In BH, circumstancial clauses may be both *verbal or *nominal and almost always begin with a *waw. Joüon §159; GKC §156.

citation formula. *n.* Any idiom or construction used to cite another literary source, which is often found in an interrogative form, such as in Joshua 10:13: הֲלֹא־הִיא כְתוּבָה עַל־סֵפֶר הַיָּשָׁר, "Is it not written in the Book of Yashar?" GKC §150e.

clash. *n.* In phonology, the overlapping of particular sounds, especially across related dialects. The ד in Aramaic and the ז in BH clash in some cognate terms, such as Aramaic דהב, "gold," and BH זהב, "gold." Homonymic clash is the appearance of two likesounding words in similar contexts.

class noun. *n.* A noun used to refer to any class or particular grouping of entities. In BH, it is often found with the definite article, but not always. Class nouns are usually found in the singular and have a *collective nuance to them (e.g., Ex 24:4: וּשְׁתֵּים עֶשְׂרֵה מַצֵּבָה, lit.

"and twelve *pillar*"). See also collective noun; singulative.

Classical Biblical Hebrew. *n.* The BH of the Israelite period in ancient Palestine, which is represented in the preexilic prose material of the Hebrew Bible. The term *Classical Hebrew* has also been more broadly used for BH at times. MNK §2.1. *See also* Late Biblical Hebrew.

classical fallacy. *n.* The erroneous assumption that older is better in language, especially when traditional grammarians identify colloquial simplification as a degeneration of classical language. Modern linguistics, being primarily descriptive, generally rejects prescriptive value judgments.

classical grammar. *n.* The traditional study and instruction in language, which is prescriptive in approach. It is to be contrasted with modern linguistic method, which is more descriptive. In other words, it is focused on what actually does happen in a language or languages in general. Classical grammar is far more concerned with judgments about "right" and "wrong" construction. Originally, grammar, rhetoric and literary criticism were inseparable from philosophy. Plato and Aristotle both made some of the most basic distinctions, and further development was made by the Stoic school and especially by Dyonysius Thrax in the second century B.C.

classical period. *n.* The era of preexilic BH literary composition.

classical Semitic languages. *n.* A term sometimes employed to refer to premodern literary Semitic languages such as BH, *Syriac, *Arabic and * Geʿez.

clausal adverbs. *n.* Adverbs that modify the verbal action on the clause level rather than just on the word level. These exert influence over the entire clause. A good example of clausal adverbs are *interrogative particles.

clausal apposition. *See* apposition.

clause. *n.* The most basic form of a complete thought, whether all or part of a complete sentence. Unlike a phrase, it has a subject and a predicate; however, it may be either nominal or verbal. There are three basic types of clauses: main clause (can stand as an independent sentence); subordinate clause (cannot stand independently but relies on a main clause to make sense); and coordinate clause. Joüon §153; MNK §12; GKC §140; *IBHS* §4.3.

climactic parallelism. *n.* A literary construction that uses parallelism in a stepladder type of pattern to the climax of the thought. Also called stairlike, repetitive, or chain-figure parallelism. Joel 1:4 offers an example (NASB):

> What the gnawing locust has left, the *swarming locust* has eaten;
>
> And what the *swarming locust* has left, the creeping locust has eaten;
>
> And what the creeping locust has left, the stripping locust has eaten.

climax. *See* peak.

closed syllable. *n.* A syllable in which a vowel is enclosed by two consonants (CVC). *See also* open syllable; half-closed syllable; doubly closed syllable.

closed vowel. *n.* A vowel value that is pronounced by keeping the mouth as closed as possible.

coalesce. *v.* To grow together. In linguistic studies, coalescence often refers to how two vowels merged together but may also be used for other modifications, such as assimilation.

codex. *n.* An ancient manuscript bound in folio leaves (a book) rather than as a scroll. *pl.* codices.

codex rescriptus. *See* palimpsest.

codices. *See* codex.

cognate. *adj.* Pertaining to words or languages that have developed from a common ancestor.

cognate accusative. *n.* (1) The use of a noun of the same root as the verb to provide clarity or emphasis; also referred to as an absolute object, internal object, internal accusative, *schema etymologicum* or *figura etymologica* (e.g., Ex 32:30: אַתֶּם חֲטָאתֶם חֲטָאָה, "You have sinned a sin." (2) Some grammarians also use this nomenclature to refer to the cognate infinitive absolute used with a finite verb. In these cases the infinitive absolute is used to intensify the action (e.g., Gen 2:17b: כִּי בְּיוֹם אֲכָלְךָ מִמֶּנּוּ מוֹת תָּמוּת, "because in the day you eat of it, *you will most definitely die*") Many grammarians now judiciously reject this nomenclature, based upon the fact that the cognate infinitive absolute does not function as an accusative (a verbal object). GKC §117p-r.

cognate object. *See* cognate accusative.

cognate verbal complement. *See* cognate accusative (2).

coherence. *See* cohesion.

cohesion. *n.* The interrelation of the various parts (grammatical and syntactical) of a text and their contribution to the progression of the discourse and unity of thought.

cohortative. *n.* A *volitive mood in BH and the Northwest Semitic languages formed from the *prefix conjugation (e.g., Ugaritic CTA 23:1: *iqra ilim nᶜmm*, "I will invoke the gracious gods"). In BH it functions similarly to the *jussive but is limited to the first person. It is frequently indistinguishable from the regular prefix conjugation except by context. However, it often takes a lengthened form with the suffix הָ (*cohortative *he*). Like the jussive, it is often accompanied by the emphatic particle נָא. Joüon §§45, 114; MNK §§15.4, 19.4; GKC §§48, 108; *IBHS* §34.5. *See also* volitive moods; jussive.

co-hyponyms. *n.* Two or more words that have a similar relationship to a *superordinate. A superordinate would be something of a larger classification (e.g., a tree) and may have multiple *hyponyms (e.g., oak, maple, birch). The relationship between hyponyms is termed co-hyponymy.

coinage. *n.* The invention of a new word or words.

cola. *See* colon.

collation. *n.* Within the discipline of textual criticism, the gathering and comparing of variant manuscript readings for the reconstruction of a text closer to that of "the original."

collective noun. *n.* A noun that is morphologically singular in form but indicates plurality; also referred to as a collective singular. It may be used with a plural verb without being considered a breach in grammatical *concord. For example, עוֹף can be translated "bird" or "birds" (Gen 1:26). GKC §123.

collective singular. *See* collective noun.

collocation. *n.* A pair of words sharing either *paradigmatic relations (e.g., stone and wall) or words in a sentence sharing *syntagmatic relations (e.g., "mow" and "lawn" in "He mowed the lawn").

colloquial. *adj.* Typical of common speech, often relaxed or informal and inappropriate in certain contexts.

colloquialism. *n.* An informal expression of common speech usually discouraged in formal settings and documents (e.g., *y'all* from *you all*, which should be simply *you*).

colon. *n.* A single line of poetic verse; also traditionally referred to as a *stich or *hemistich. *pl.* cola. *See also* bicolon; tricolon.

colophon. *n.* An inscription at the end of a document indicating authorship, place and date of publication, or any other pertinent information that the author deems necessary, including in some cases an *imprecation.

comedy. *n.* In classical *literary criticism, a story that has a happy ending. Usually it begins in prosperity, dips to *tragedy and rises again to prosperity, or it may just move from tragedy to felicity.

comitative. *adj.* Pertaining to a grammatical construction, usually employing a preposition, that conveys the joining of two or more things by association. In English the idea is expressed by the preposition "with" or the conjunctive "also." In BH it is most often expressed by the preposition עִם but frequently by the *beth comitantiae.

command. *See* imperative.

comment. *n.* (1) The sentence construction defining the topic in a *topic-comment construction. (2) A parenthetic statement often expressing the personal opinion of the speaker.

common. *adj.* In Semitic grammar, referring to pronominal or verbal person markers that are gender neutral and thus may have either a masculine or feminine noun as referent.

commutation. *n.* (1) A consonantal change from a harder to a softer sound, such as when a *dagesh forte* is omitted in a form for the smoothing of pronunciation. In the MT this is often marked by a *raphe, a short horizontal accent stroke over the top. (2) The reduction of one letter to a softer letter of *homogeneous or *homorganic nature, such as the צ in צָחַק being changed to שׂ in שׂחק.

compaginis **letter.** *n.* An extant letter left over from obsolete Semitic case endings.

comparative clause. *n.* A subordinate clause that compares one entity with another. *See also* comparative degree.

comparative degree. *n.* An expression comparing one thing with another. In English it is expressed by the suffix "-er" and the words "than" and "more than." In BH it is expressed by the use of the *comparative *min* (מִן) "than." Joüon §141; MNK §30.5; GKC §133; IBHS §14.4. *See also* degree; positive degree; superlative degree.

comparative linguistics. *n.* The descriptive study of language by comparative method; previously known as comparative philology.

comparative *min.* *n.* The use of the preposition מִן to express the idea of "than," as in "greater than" or "stronger than." The preposition may function as either a *free or a *bound morpheme. As a bound morpheme, it becomes a preformative and the *nun* assimilates (e.g., Is 55:9: כִּי־גָבְהוּ שָׁמַיִם מֵאָרֶץ כֵּן גָּבְהוּ דְרָכַי מִדַּרְכֵיכֶם, "For as the heavens are higher *than* the earth, so are my ways higher *than* your ways"). Joüon §174; GKC §161.

comparative philology. *n.* A late-eighteenth to early-nineteenth century term originally used to refer to the scientific historical study of language grammar among languages of similar and divergent phylum. Also called comparative grammar or comparative historical linguistics, it was one of the major steps in the modern scientific investigation of language (modern linguistics), in contrast to the prescriptive approaches of classical grammar. *See also* comparative linguistics.

compensative lengthening. *See* compensatory lengthening.

compensatory lengthening. *n.* The lengthening of a vowel due to the refusal of the following *consonant to receive a *dagesh forte* because it is a *guttural letter. This applies to *resh* and all gutturals except for ה and ח, which are considered *doubled by implication. In BH, *patach* (ַ) becomes *qamets* (ָ); *hireq* (ִ) becomes *tsere* (ֵ); and *qibbuts* (ֻ) becomes *holem* (ֹ).

complement. *n.* A necessary constituent of a sentence to complete a *verbal predicate; the *objective accusative of a transitive verb. This is to be distinguished from an *adjunct, which is an *optional constituent (adverbial accusative). In English grammar, a word, phrase or clause that completes the meaning of the predicate is considered a complement, and a further distinction is made between an object complement and a subject complement. The object complement further clarifies the direct object (e.g., "I [S] found [V] the test [DO] easy [OC]"). A subject complement further clarifies the subject (e.g., "Dr. Fields [S] became [V] president [SC]").

complement clause. *n.* A subordinate clause that is so necessary to the meaning of the main clause that the sentence would not make sense without it. It may be either a subject or an object clause. In

" 'I have to go home,' is what he said," the clause "I have to go home" is the subject of the sentence. Contrast with *supplement clause.

complementizer. *n.* A word or clause employed to mark reported speech or another clause. *See also* embedding; quotative frame.

complete imperfect. *See* long *yiqtol*.

complex sentence. *n.* A sentence comprising a main clause and one or more subordinate clauses (e.g., Josh 4:4: "Then Joshua called the twelve men, whom he had prepared of the sons of Israel"). *See also* compound sentence.

complex word. *n.* A word that is made up of more than one morpheme. *See also* simple word.

composite *shewa.* *See* compound *shewa.*

compound-complex sentence. *n.* A sentence consisting of at least two *main clauses and at least one *subordinate clause (e.g., Ruth 1:18-19a: "And when she observed that she was resolved to accompany her, she ceased speaking to her, and the two of them continued until they came unto Bethlehem"). *See also* compound sentence; complex sentence.

compound noun. *n.* Two nouns that together make up a single concept and may be either written together or apart (e.g., "complex sentence").

compound numeral. *n.* The combining of two or more *cardinal numerals to express a larger figure, such as מֵאָה וַחֲמִשִּׁים, "one hundred and fifty."

compound prepositions. *n.* The joining of two or more prepositions together to create a compound or to strengthen meaning, such as מִן and עַל to form מֵעַל, "from above, above."

compound relative pronoun. *n.* A pronoun made up of a *relative pronoun plus the word *ever* (e.g., whoever, whatever, whenever).

compound sentence. *n.* A sentence made up of two or more *main or *independent clauses. In BH, compound sentences may be classified into four categories: *conjunctive, *chiastic, *contrastive and *antithetical. They are also common in BH poetry. GKC §143.

compound *shewa.* *n.* BH vowel *qualities formed by compounding the simple *vocal *shewa* with a *full vowel sign; also called half-vowels or *hateph* vowels. The value is still only a half-vowel; therefore, they cannot form a stand-alone *syllable but must al-

ways accompany a full vowel. They are preferred by *guttural letters and include: *hateph patach (ֲ); *hateph qamets (ֳ); and *hateph
segol (ֱ). Joüon §§8-9; MNK §8.1; GKC §10. See also silent shewa; vocal shewa.

compound subject. n. Two or more nouns acting as a subject for a
single verb, such as, "The dog and the cat were sleeping on the
porch." GKC §146.

compound syllable. See closed syllable.

compound verb. n. A verb whose meaning and force is strength-
ened by a preposition.

comprehensive locative. n. A locative grammatical element that expresses an expansive or comprehensive locus of reference. In BH it
is often expressed by עַל, "above," or מֵעַל, "from above."

conative. adj. Pertaining to expressions in which an addressor at-
tempts to cause an addressee to do as he or she wishes.

concatenation. n. The joining of a group of *immediate constituents
into a chain, such as a construct relationship; also referred to as
chaining.

concept. n. In semantics, the thing to which a word (sign) refers; also
called a referent. Linguists make a distinction between a sign versus a referent or a word versus a concept. See also sign; referent;
concept analysis.

concept analysis. n. The study of a concept, in contrast to a word
study. There is a fundamental distinction between word usage and
concept. This is made most clear by how a single word may be
used in reference to different concepts. See also sign; referent; concept.

concessive clause. n. A *subordinate clause that concedes a fact in
relation to the *main clause. It is marked by a number of possible
*particles, which can be translated "though," "unless" or "al-
though," including the *waw-conjunctive, עַל, גַּם, כִּי, אִם, and כִּ
(e.g., Is 1:15: גַּם כִּי־תַרְבּוּ תְפִלָּה אֵינֶנִּי שֹׁמֵעַ, "Although you multiply
prayers, I will not listen"). Joüon §171; GKC §160.

concord. n. The rule in language that certain parts of speech must
possess a grammatical congruity with one another to be joined in
a syntactic relationship. Also called agreement, congruence or
grammatical concord. For example, דִּבֶּר הָאִישׁ, "The man spoke,"
is a third masculine singular verb with a *masculine *singular

noun. Joüon §§148-152; GKC §145.

concrete noun. *n.* A noun that refers to a tangible thing such as a hand, foot, man, woman or tree. Contrast with *abstract nouns (e.g., love, joy, peace, strength, virtue). *See also* animate; nonanimate.

conditional clause. *See* protasis.

conditional sentence. A sentence made up of a conditional dependent clause (*protasis) followed by a main clause (*apodosis). The apodosis states that a certain action will materialize, conditioned upon the materialization of another state or action (protasis). In Genesis 18:3, אִם־נָא מָצָאתִי חֵן בְּעֵינֶיךָ, "If now I have found favor in your sight," is the protasis, while אַל־נָא תַעֲבֹר מֵעַל עַבְדֶּךָ, "please do not pass your servant by," is the apodosis. Joüon §167; GKC §159.

conflation. *n.* In text-critical investigation, the redactional synthesizing of two different readings of a text.

conflict. *n.* The fundamental problem established early in a story that moves toward *resolution over the course of a *narrative.

conflict resolution. *See* resolution.

congener. *n.* In comparative linguistics, a language derived from the same genus or language *phylum as other related languages.

congruence. *See* concord.

conjugation. *n.* An orderly arrangement of *inflected verbal forms organized according to the various elements, such as *aspect, *tense, *voice, *mood, *gender and *number. In the historic study of BH grammar, since the time of J. Reuchlin, the term has more narrowly been associated with the *derived stems.

conjunction. *n.* A syntactical element employed to relate words or clauses. There are two types of conjunctions: coordinating and subordinating. Coordinating conjunctions *(and, but, or, nor)* join words, phrases or clauses of equal standing. Subordinating conjunctions *(if, that, because, since)* introduce a subordinate clause (e.g., "He came inside *because* he was hungry"). While BH has a number of conjunctives, it usually employs the *waw* for both coordination and subordination. Joüon §§104, 115-120; MNK §§21, 40; GKC §§104, 111-112; *IBHS* §§32-33. *See also* weqatal; wayyiqtol.

conjunctive. *adj.* Pertaining to grammatical, syntactical or phonological coordination.

conjunctive accent. *n.* *An accent of the *masoretic pointing system that joins words together in pronunciation. *See also* accent.

conjunctive adverb. *n.* An *adverb that functions like a conjunction in that it links the actions of two or more independent clauses (e.g., *indeed, then, hence, therefore, accordingly, however, thus, besides*).

conjunctive *dagesh forte. See dagesh forte* euphonic.

conjunctive sentence. *n.* One of the four types of BH *compound sentences. It is simply coordinated by the *waw*-conjunctive and is employed for various *parallelisms. *See also* chiastic sentence; contrastive sentence; antithetic sentence.

conjunctivi. See conjunctive accent.

connecting vowel. *n.* A vowel used in the morphological process of attaching a *consonantal suffix to a noun or verb to prevent the *juxtaposition of two consonants. *See also* linking condition.

connective. *n.* Any morpheme that creates a syntactical relationship, such as an *adverb, *conjunction or *particle.

connotation. *n.* The subjective meaning attached to word that is not inherent in the word itself but tends to arise from social experience and customs (e.g., the negative ideas often associated with the word *stepmother* because of the story of Cinderella). *See also* denotation.

consectio temporum. See consecution; *waw*-consecutive.

consecution. *n.* (1) A series or arrangement in linear succession. In BH this may refer to a successive string of accents. (2) More often, the *waw*-consecutive narration in both the *prefix and *suffix conjugations.

consecutive clause. *See* result clause.

consequential independent clause. *See* apodosis.

conservatism. *n.* In linguistics, the tendency of a language or family of languages to retain long-standing words and constructions. *See also* innovation.

consonant. *n.* Like the related term *vowel*, the term *consonant* is ill-defined in traditional grammar. For the linguist, consonants are defined according to their phonetic value, which leads to a plethora of sub-phonetic classifications, including *voiced versus *unvoiced; *oral versus *nasal; and *stops versus *plosives. GKC §§5-6.

consonantal suffix. *See* heavy consonantal suffix; light consonantal suffix.

constative. *adj.* Any element that continues in a particular state.

constituent. *See* syntagm.

construct chain. *See* construct state.

construct infinitive. *See* infinitive construct.

construct noun. *n.* The governing word of a construct relationship followed by the *absolute noun. *See also* construct state.

construct override. *See* broken construct chain.

construct phrase. *n.* A genitival phrase governed by a construct noun. *See* construct state.

construct relationship. *See* construct state.

construct state. *n.* In the Semitic languages in general, the joining of nouns into a *genitival relationship by the use of *juxtaposition and a *linking condition. Such linking conditions are created usually by *proclisis and vowel reduction. There may be from two to four words participating in the formation of a construct chain. The last word of the chain is always in the *absolute state (e.g., בֵּית דָּוִד, "house of David." Joüon §§92, 129; MNK §§25.1-26.2; GKC §§89, 128; *IBHS* §9.

constructio ad sensum. Lat. "construction according to the sense." *See also* ad sensum; pregnant construction.

constructio praegnans. *See* pregnant construction.

content word. *n.* A word with lexical meaning, in contrast to a *form word.

context. *n.* The broader background of a discourse in which a particular utterance or statement is set or the sense (meaning) of a particular statement as interpreted in light of its historical situation. *See also* text; co-text.

contextual. *adj.* Pertaining to *context.

contingency. *n.* The dependency of the results of one verbal action upon another action or circumstance, as in a *conditional sentence.

contingent locative. *n.* A locative grammatical construction indicating "at," "by" or "next to." *See also* locative; locative *he*.

continuant. *n.* Speech sounds for which the airflow is never fully restricted during pronunciation; also referred to as spirants. These may be perpetually pronounced until the speaker is out of breath. There are three basic types of continuants: *nasal, *lateral and *fricative.

continuative. *See* linear action.

contraction. *n.* The dropping, coalescing or *assimilating of letters in the creation of new word forms. This is done for the purpose of smoothing pronunciation.

contraries. *n.* A class of antonyms that are juxtapositional opposites (e.g., short or tall).

contrastive analysis. *n.* In comparative linguistics, the study of dialects, discrete languages or families of languages with regard to their differences.

contrastive sentence. *n.* A compound sentence in which the two clauses are set to contrast each other, such as Genesis 3:15b: הוּא יְשׁוּפְךָ רֹאשׁ וְאַתָּה תְּשׁוּפֶנּוּ עָקֵב, "He will bruise your *head*, but you will bruise his *heel*." See also antithetic sentence; conjunctive sentence; chiastic sentence.

converted imperfect. *See wayyiqtol.*

converted perfect. *See weqatal.*

coordinate clause. *n.* One of two equal clauses in a compound sentence that are related by a conjunction.

coordinate conjunction. *See* conjunction.

coordinate relationship. *n.* (1) Used loosely, any type of syntactical coordination by use of *conjunctions, *conjunctive adverbs, *parataxis or *asyndeton. (2) The coordination of two or more verbs by the use of a *waw-consecutive, in which the first verb has a governing power over the consecutive verbs in the sequence in regard to mood and aspect. *See also wayyiqtol.*

coordination. *n.* The relating of one sentence element to another, usually by means of a coordinating *conjunction or by simple *parataxis.

Copper Scroll. *n.* A unique scroll found in Cave 1 at Qumran that was inscribed on copper but contained no biblical text.

copula. *n.* A word that links sentence elements in order to create predication in a nominal clause. These verbs are also referred to as linking verbs, equative verbs, binders, *existential particles or verbs of being. BH sometimes uses the verb הִיה, "to be, exist," as a copular verb. In most cases in BH, a verb of being is implied, such as in Deuteronomy 4:35: כִּי יְהוָה הוּא הָאֱלֹהִים, "because YHWH he is the Elohim." The term can also be used more broadly for conjunctions. Joüon §154i-j; GKC §141g-i; *IBHS* §8.4. *See also* predicate adjective; copula.

copular. *adj.* Pertaining to a copula or any form of syntactical joining.

copulative predicate. *See* predicate nominative.

copulative *waw*. *See waw*-consecutive.

conversive. *adj.* In the study of semantics, relating to the occurrence of binary terms that are considered the reverse of the other, such as husband and wife or בּוֹא, "come in," and יָצָא, "go out."

conversive *waw*. *See waw*-consecutive.

co-referent. *See* antecedent.

co-referential. *adj.* Pertaining to two or more words that relate to the same extralinguistic entity, that is, a referent.

correlative conjunction. *n.* A conjunction that correlates sentence elements (e.g., *neither, nor, either, or, both*).

correspondence. *n.* In comparative phonetics, the interrelationship of phonemes across various dialects of a certain language phylum; also referred to as phonetic clash or crash. Joüon §5r.

co-text. *n.* Other discourse units surrounding the discourse that is the object of study. These discourse units are an integral part of macrosyntactical structure and the semantics of the target discourse (e.g., Gen 1:1—2:3 and 3:1-24 are co-texts for Gen 2:4-25). *See also* text; context.

count noun. *n.* A noun that may indicate a single entity (e.g., boy, girl, tree, ball), in contrast to a *mass noun.

countable. *See* count noun.

counter-tone. *n.* A secondary accentual stress upon a word. *See also meteg.*

couplet. *See* bicolon.

covenant lawsuit. *n.* A subgenre of prophetic-type literature in the Hebrew Bible in which God's prophet is sent as a prosecuting attorney delivering an indictment against the people of God (see, e.g., Ps 50; Is 1:2-9; Jer 2:4-13; Hos 4:1-10; Mic 6:1-8). This subgenre is also referred to as the *rib* pattern, based upon the use of the term רִיב, "to contend, bring an indictment."

credo. *See* creedal statement.

creedal statement. *n.* A short statement in the Hebrew Bible or any religious text that has a confessional tone and is characterized by historical elements that are central to the shape of that faith. Gerhard von Rad pointed to Deuteronomy 6:20-24 and 26:5b-10a as examples of creedal statements.

crux interpretum. n. Specifically, a text-critical problem that is un-
solvable, though it may be used more broadly for any interpretive
problem.

cuneiform. n. One of the earliest writing systems. This "wedge-
shaped writing" was developed by the *Sumerians in the third
millennium B.C. and employed in Mesopotamia until the first century A.D. It was adopted for many languages in the ancient Near
East, such as *Akkadian, *Hittite and *Persian. The system is composed of hundreds of signs that are either syllabic (representative
of syllables) or ideographic (representative of ideas). *See also*
Ugaritic.

Cushitic. adj. Outdated nomenclature to describe the languages of
East Africa, such as Somali and Oromo, which are now generally
classed as *Afroasiatic.

customary action. *See* iterative.

D

D. n. An abbreviation for Deuteronomist or the Deuteronomic
source document, especially the Deuteronomic Code (Deut 12—
26). *See also* JEDP theory.

D stem. n. A common Semitic verbal inflection characterized by a
"doubling" (hence the D) of the *medial consonant. In BH, the D
stem is traditionally referred to as the Piel, in Aramaic and Syriac
as the Pael.

dagesh. n. BH דָּגֵשׁ, "piercing." —A dot placed in a Hebrew letter to
harden or double its pronunciation. *Dagesh lene* appears in the six
begadkepat letters and hardens their pronunciation (e.g., בּ = v, and
בּ = b). *Dagesh forte* doubles a letter's value (e.g., קִטֵּל in the Piel
stem = קְטֵל). A *begadkepat* letter can take both a *dagesh lene* or a
dagesh forte. Discerning between them requires an understanding
of BH *syllable structure. Non-*begadkepat* letters can take only a
dagesh forte, and *gutturals and the letter *resh* can never take one
because they reject being doubled, which results in *compensatory
lengthening. GKC §§12-13, 20; MNK §8.2.

dagesh forte. See *dagesh.*

dagesh forte affectuosum. n. The use of a *dagesh* to make a vowel especially emphatic. This usually occurs in *pause (e.g., Judg 5:7: חָדְל֫וּ). GKC §20i.

dagesh forte characteristic. *See dagesh forte characteristicum.*

dagesh forte characteristicum. *n.* The characteristic employment of a *dagesh forte* in a particular verbal conjugation (i.e., Piel, Pual and Hithpael). GKC §20a. *See also dagesh.*

dagesh forte compensative. *n.* The representation of two consonants (usually identical but not always) by a single form of the letter pointed with the *dagesh forte* (doubling). This also sometimes accompanies assimilation. For example, when the preposition מִן is added to the beginning of a word, it assimilates the *nun* into the first root letter in the form of a *dagesh forte* (For example, כֹּל plus מִן produces the hypothetical form מִנְכֹּל, which is written as מִכֹּל). GKC §20a. *See also dagesh.*

dagesh forte conjunctive. *n.* The use of a *dagesh forte* to unite two words in pronunciation. Joüon §18; GKC §20c. *See also dagesh.*

dagesh forte delitescens. *See dagesh forte implicitum.*

dagesh forte dirimens. *n.* A euphonic use of *dagesh forte* to separate syllables for the sake smoothing pronunciation by causing a *silent shewa* to become vocal. This is usually caused by the quality of the consonant, most often a sonant (i.e., liquid), sibilant or emphatic *qoph* (e.g., Lev 25:5: עִנְּבֵי instead of עִנְבֵי). Joüon §18k; GKC §20h.

dagesh forte euphonic. *n.* A *dagesh forte* placed in the initial consonant of a word to link it phonetically to the preceding word, usually for smoothing pronunciation. This is generally preceded by a *maqqeph*. Joüon §18; GKC §20c.

dagesh forte firmativum. *n.* The use of a *dagesh forte* for strengthening the pronunciation of the consonants ל, נ and מ, as in the independent pronouns הֵנָּה, הֵמָּה and אֵלֶּה. GKC §20k.

dagesh forte implicitum. *n.* A case in which *dagesh forte* is understood but not graphically represented. This occurs primarily in the letters ה and ח, sometimes in ע, and seldom in א. GKC §§20m, 22c. *See also* implicit doubling.

dagesh forte occultum. *See dagesh forte implicitum.*

dagesh lene. *n.* A dagesh placed in the tenues (*begadkepat* letters) that causes a hardening of the consonantal sound but does not double the letter's value, as does *dagesh forte.*

dagesh necessarium. *See dagesh forte compensative.*

dagesh orthophonicum. *See orthophonic dagesh.*

dangling letters. *See* suspended letters.

dangling participle. *n.* A participle used as a nominative absolute. *See also casus pendens.*

dative case. *n.* The case of the *indirect object; also known as the case of reception. It usually expresses "to" or "toward." BH has no dative case ending, but it, like all languages, has the dative case function, often expressed through the inseparable preposition לְ, "to."

datives commodi et incommodi. *See lamed* of interest.

dativus ethicus. *See* ethical dative.

deadjectival. *adj.* Pertaining to a nominal derived from an *adjective.

deaspiration. *n.* A letter's loss of its *aspiration in pronunciation. *See also* spirantization.

Decalogue. *n.* The *Septuagint's nomenclature for the Ten Commandments (Gk. "Ten Words"), found in Exodus 20:1-17 and Deuteronomy 5:6-21.

dechiq. Aramaic דְּחִיק, "compressed." —*n.* A situation in which a word ends in a *mater lectionis* ה and is followed by an accented monosyllabic word or a word accented on the first syllable. In such cases, the preceding word loses its own accent and is joined by *maqqeph,* and the initial consonant of the following word is *doubled by a conjunctive *dagesh forte.* Because of this change in accent (lack of stress on the vowel followed by the ה), the vowel is considered to be "compressed" (as ancient Jewish grammarians called it), and the two words are pronounced together (e.g., לְכָה־נָּא, "come now," pronounced lekan-na, not lekah-na). Note that the ה becomes *quiescent and has no consonantal value. Joüon §18i; GKC §20c. *See also* athe merachiq.

declarative. *See* indicative.

declarative-estimative. *See* delocutive.

declarative sentence. *See* sentence.

declension. *n.* The systematic organization of the all possible inflectional forms of a noun, pronoun, adjective or participle.

decompose. *v.* To analyze grammatical units or break units down from sentences to words to morphemes.

deep structure. *n.* The underlying sentence structure, as contrasted with surface structure. While two sentences' surface structures may seem very divergent, they may have very similar or identical deep structure and vice versa. It is founded upon the underlying internal network of relationships between words and ideas. *See also* surface structure.

deesis. *n.* Invoking the name of a deity or other authoritative thing in the process of making a plea: "In the name of God, please stop!"

defective verbs. *n.* Verbs similar to each other in consonants and meaning and in which the conjugations or tenses are borrowed and exchanged in the process of inflection. In other words, some verbal inflections come from one root word, while other inflections for the same basic meaning come from the other root word. For example, the root טוב will be used for some expressions of the idea "to do or be good," but for others the root יטב will be used to convey the idea "to be good." Joüon §85.

defective writing. *n.* Omission of a *mater lectionis* in a word that typically has it. Before the *masoretic pointing system was devised for the Hebrew Bible, a cruder system of vowel indication used certain Hebrew consonants as vowel letters or *matres lectionis* ("mothers of reading"). When a word that commonly has a *mater* is found without it, grammarians refer to it as defective writing or *scriptio defectiva*. *See also* full writing.

definite. *n.* A word that is particular, most often accompanied by a definite article (e.g., "the stone"). Proper names and nouns are definite by implication and thus do not require a definite article. *See also* indefinite; articular; anarthrous.

definite accusative. *See* direct-object marker.

definite direct-object marker. See direct-object marker.

definite numeral adjective. *See* adjective.

deflection. *See* imale.

degeminate. *See* degemination.

degemination. *n.* The reduction of a *geminate (i.e., a doubled consonant) back to a single consonantal value.

degree. *n.* The differentiation of three basic levels of attributive quality: *positive or absolute degree (good); *comparative degree (better); and *superlative degree (best). Joüon §141; MNK §30.5; GKC §133; *IBHS* §14.4-5.

deictic element. *n.* A free or bound *morpheme that defines spatiotemporal and social relationships. *See also* deixis; anaphora; cataphora.

deictics. *n.* The study of discourse deixis.

deixis. *n.* The spatiotemporal, personal, social, discourse and locative relationships in an utterance.

deliberative. *adj.* Of clausal constructions that pertain to making a decision.

delocutive. *adj.* Referring to the formal affirmation of a state of being (already existing) rather than identifying the creation of a state, such as the *factitive.

demonstrative adverb. *n.* A particle that acts as a pointer toward the action of the verb. Common demonstrative adverbial particles in BH are כֹּה and כֵּן, often translated "thus," "so" or "according."

demonstrative element. *n.* Any grammatical element that has the feature of pointing, specifying or making definite, including definite articles, all demonstrative pronouns and the demonstrative element *he.*

demonstrative he. *n.* The BH definite article. Earlier Hebrew grammarians used the term *demonstrative* because of its pointing function. In BA, the suffixed letter ה is used to indicate "this, that" (e.g., Dan 5:30: בֵּהּ בְּלֵילְיָא, "In *that* night").

demonstrative pronoun. *n.* A *deictic element that points out persons, places or things. It may function as a predicative and an attributive adjective. BH, like English, has two classes of demonstratives: *near demonstratives ("this, these") and *far demonstratives ("that, those"). Joüon §§36, 143; MNK §36.2; GKC §§34, 136; *IBHS* §17.

denominal. *See* denominative.

denominative. *n.* A verb that was derived from a noun. For example, אָהַל, "to camp," is derived from the noun אֹהֶל, "tent." *See also* deverbative.

denotation. *n.* The commonly accepted meaning of a word as it points to an extralinguistic entity (*referent). It is contrasted with *connotation, which is the subjective meaning a word takes on from usage or social contexts.

dental plosives. *n.* A dental consonant that is pronounced by a blast of air (*plosive): ת, ט, ד, ד. *See also* dentals.

dentals. *n.* The consonants pronounced by pressing the tongue against the upper teeth or *alveolar ridge, causing a brief restriction in the airflow: ת, ט, ד, ד, ל, נ and ר (rolled). MNK §4.2.4ii.

dento-alveolars. *See* dentals.

dependent clause. *n.* A subordinate clause. *See also* clause.

dependent personal pronouns. *n.* *Anaphora that may not stand on their own but function as *bound morphemes by being suffixed to the words they modify. They may be bound to nouns or verbs.

depharyngealization. *n.* The process by which *pharyngeal letters (ח, ע, ק) increasingly have lost their pharyngeal value.

derivation. *n.* The origination and formation of words, as distinguished from inflexion (*morphology).

derivational affixes. *n.* *Bound morphemes that indicate word class. They may identify a word as an adjective, noun and so on. Much of BH's derivational modification, as with other Semitic languages, is accomplished by vowel-stem modification and consonantal *affixes.

derivatives. *See* derived conjugations.

derived conjugations. *n.* In Semitic languages, verbal-stem conjugations that are derived from the ground stem. For example, a derivative stem of the ground stem קדשׁ is the Hithpael התקדשׁ. In BH, the ground stem is the Qal, and the derived stems are the Niphal, Piel, Pual and so forth. The ground stem in BA is the Peal, and the derivatives include the Peil, Hithpeel, Pael and Haphel.

descriptive adjective. *See* attributive adjective.

descriptive linguistics. *See* linguistics.

desiderative clause. *n.* A clause that expresses a wish or a desire. This is customarily expressed by use of the volitive moods, such as the jussive, in Semitic languages. GKC §151.

desiderative mood. *See* volitive moods.

determinant, determination. *n.* (1) The third radical of the triliteral root. (2) Sometimes a reference to definiteness. *See also* determinate state.

determinate. *See* determinate state; definite.

determinate state. A word definite by implication or by a grammatical construction. In BH this can be accomplished in several ways: (1) prefixing of the definite article; (2) addition of a pronominal suffix; or (3) placement in construct with a definite absolute noun.

Basic determination is formed by adding a definite article: in BH, ה plus a *dagesh forte* in the initial root consonant; in BA, the definite article suffix (א). Joüon §§35, 137; MNK §24.4; GKC §§35, 125-127; IBHS §13. *See also* indeterminate.

Deutero-Isaiah. *n.* The nomenclature in biblical criticism normally assigned to Isaiah 40—66; for those who propose a *Trito-Isaiah, more narrowly Isaiah 40—55; also known as Second Isaiah.

deuterocanonical. *adj.* Historically, pertaining to the *Apocrypha, but generally, for any class of writings that has a secondary relationship to a central and fixed *canon.

Deuteronomic, Deuteronomistic. *adj.* Though sometimes used interchangeably, these terms are independent and specific. In the classic schema of Martin Noth, *Deuteronomic* refers to material derived from a preexilic Ur-Deuteronomy (UrDt), which was probably authored during the Josianic reforms of the seventh century B.C.; *Deuteronomistic* refers to material derived from an exilic-period revision at the hands of a *redactor (Dtr).

Deuteronomist. *n.* (1) According to Martin Noth and criticism in general today, the proposed exilic author of the *Deuteronomistic History (Deuteronomy—2 Kings). (2) In the traditional Graf-Wellhausen school, the author of Deuteronomy and like material. *See also* JEDP.

Deuteronomistic History. *n.* In OT criticism this refers to Deuteronomy—2 Kings, which is viewed as a single composition by an exilic author who purportedly lived in Palestine. Simply put, it is characterized by a theological perspective on the history of Israel that judges Israel according to its faithfulness to the covenant as presented in Deuteronomy.

Deuteronomistic Redactor. *n.* Abbreviated Dtr. *See* Deuteronomist.

deverbative. *n.* A noun that was derived from a verb. *See also* denominative.

deviation. *n.* Any break in linguistic or stylistic patterns.

diachronic. *adj.* (1) Relating to any method of historical inquiry that studies more than one epoch of time at once. (2) In the study of modern linguistics, pertaining to the study of a language over the history of its existence. It is to be contrasted with *synchronic *linguistics, which focuses on a particular era.

diachronic linguistics. *n.* The descriptive study of a language over the various periods of its existence. *See also* synchronic linguistics.

dialect. *n.* A branch of a language with its own personal developments and idiosyncrasies.

dialect geography. *n.* The study of languages and dialects in the context of their geographical proximity or the study of regional dialects.

dialectology. *See* dialect geography.

diaphora. *n.* The repetitive use of a word in a discourse or utterance but with a slight change of meaning in each occurrence.

diconsonantal root. *See* biliteral root.

didactic. *adj.* Anything pertaining to teaching or instruction.

didactic literature. *n.* A genre of literature composed for teaching and instruction. Literary scholars often point to Deuteronomy and Proverbs as having didactic qualities.

diminution. *n.* Belittlement or description of something as small, such as is found with the use of a *diminutive morpheme.

diminutive. *adj.* Pertaining to an indication of youthfulness or smallness in stature, size or respect. English speakers add the diminutive sufformative *y* (e.g., Tom becomes Tommy). In BH, the suffix וֹן is added to a word to express diminution (e.g., אִישׁ, "man," becomes אִישׁוֹן, "little man").

diphthong. *n.* A single vowel sound formed of two independent vowels joined together. *See also* monophthong.

diptote. *n.* A noun inflected by only two possible case endings, as some Ugaritic nouns. *See also* diptotic.

diptotic. *adj.* Relating to a two-case structure of *nominal *inflection found in some Semitic languages. Some Ugaritic nouns are diptotic, having a nominative represented with -*u (rapanu)* and both genitive and accusative with -*a (rapana)*. *See also* triptote ; triptotic.

direct accusative. *See* direct object.

direct address. *See* direct discourse.

direct discourse. *n.* An exact quotation of the speaker's words; also called direct quotation. In English it is identified by the use of quotation marks and in most languages by a statement such as, "He said 'X.' " It may be contrasted with *indirect discourse, which is essentially a paraphrase.

direct equivalence. *n.* A theory of text translation that assumes a one-to-one translation correspondence is possible in order to provide a "literal" translation.

direct object. *n.* A nominal in the accusative case receiving the action of a transitive verb. In BH it is often marked by the *direct object marker, אֵת. Joüon §125. *See also* indirect object.

direct speech. *See* direct discourse.

direct-object marker. *n.* In BH, the particle אֵת. Traditionally known as the *nota accusatavi* ("sign of the accusative"), it is often placed before a definite direct object. The particle only carries case function and thus is untranslatable. When standing alone before the object, it is pointed as above, but when attached by a *maqqeph*, it loses its accent and undergoes a vowel reduction (אֶת־הַשָּׁמַיִם). It is also identical in form to the preposition *with* (אֵת) and should not be confused with it. Aramaic uses the ל preposition and יָת for the same function, the latter occurring only once in BA (Dan 3:12). *See also* accusative; double accusative.

direct-object pronouns. *See* object(ive) pronoun.

directional *he*. *See* locative *he*.

directive. *n.* A *performative utterance conveying the desire of the speaker to see some action committed by another; usually an *imperative or some other *volitive.

discontinuous elements. *n.* Elements of a sentence structure that deviate in some way from the standard patterns.

discord, grammatical. *n.* An inconsistency of grammar in a given language.

discourse. *n.* In modern linguistics, any block of literary composition longer than a sentence that possesses compositional and thematic unity and coherence.

discourse analysis. *n.* The disciplined analysis of a discourse unit with particular attention to structure, literary devices, motifs, themes and especially discourse semantics. This is based upon the linguistic observation that meaning is derived not only from words but also from a variety of sentential and suprasentential relationships.

discourse linguistics. *See* text linguistics.

discourse meaning. *n.* (1) The overall meaning of a *discourse in a literary composition. (2) A particular word's meaning within a discourse (connotation), as opposed to its lexical meaning (denotation).

discursive. *adj.* Pertaining to a form of speech or writing that exhibits the characteristics of narration of events; also called narrational. The term may also be used more narrowly in reference to polemical texts.

disjunctive. *adj.* Relating to any sentential element, usually a conjunction, that relates clauses by contrast, separation or the distinguishing of alternatives (e.g., *but, unless*).

disjunctive accents. *n.* Major accents of the *masoretic pointing system that are designed to separate or disjoin. For example, the *atnach is a strong disjunctive accent used to divide a Hebrew verse in half.

disjunctive clause. *n.* A clause marked by disjunctive coordination. BH disjunctive conjunctions include אִם, אוֹ and regular disjunctive וְ (e.g., 2 Sam 2:21: נְטֵה לְךָ עַל־יְמִינְךָ אוֹ עַל־שְׂמֹאלֶךָ, "turn aside to your right hand or your left hand"). Joüon §175; GKC §162. *See also* disjunctive coordination.

disjunctive coordination. *n.* An element of grammar that coordinates while communicating a contrast or distinction. In English, disjunction is expressed by the *adversatives *but* or *yet*. In BH it is most commonly indicated by the use of a clause-level *waw plus context. This is commonly referred to as a *strong disjunction (e.g., Gen 1:1-2a: "In the beginning God created the heavens and the earth, *but* the earth was without form and void").

dislocated constituent. *n.* The *nominative absolute of a *casus pendens construction.

dislocation construction. *See casus pendens.*

dissimilation. *n.* The influence of one letter upon another causing a distinguishing of the sounds. In BH, dissimilation is usually a vowel change to prevent heterogeneous vowel sounds from following one another. For example, the BH word for "beginning" is from the nominal רֹאשׁ, but when the derived word was formed the *holem was dropped for a *hireq to become רִאשׁוֹן, not רֹאשׁוֹן. Joüon §29h; GKC §27w. *See also* assimilation.

distant past. *See* pluperfect.

distribution. *n.* The possible contexts in which a linguistic unit can occur. This presupposes that there are contextual limitations on words.

distributional equivalence. *n.* When two or more words may be interchangeable or found in the same contexts.

distributional overlap. *n.* When two or more words are commonly found together as well as apart.

distributional inclusion. *n.* When one word is found only with another but not alone (e.g., *x* is found with *y*, and *y* is not found without *x*).

distributive. *adj.* Relating to something spread out over area or time (e.g., אַחַת לְשָׁלֹשׁ שָׁנִים, "once every three years").

disyllabic. *See* bisyllabic.

ditransitive. *See* double accusative; transitive verb.

dittography. *n.* A scribal error involving a duplication of a word or letter; contrast with *haplography.

document. *n.* A manuscript or text that is usually the object of study in criticism.

Documentary Hypothesis. *See* JEDP.

double accusative. *n.* The situation in which a verb governs two objects. For example, in "The people made him president," both "him" and "president" function as an *object of the verb. In BH, this phenomenon is primarily associated with but not limited to the *Hiphil and *Piel verb stems and thus may also be found with the *Qal as well. The two objects are usually placed in juxtaposition; however, they can also be separate so that one precedes the verb and the other follows (e.g., 1 Sam 8:1 [Qal]: "and he made *his sons judges*"; Deut 8:3 [Hiphil]: "and he fed *you manna*"). GKC §117cc-ll; *IBHS* §27.3a-c. *See also* accusative; undersubject; bestowal.

double conjunctions. *n.* A sentence organized with two conjunctions of identical or similar form and meaning: e.g., Lev 13:51 and Jer 32:20.

double entendre. *n.* A phrase or statement in literature which is intended to evoke more than one meaning in the mind of the reader, often to cause a level of thought and reflection. *See* wordplay.

double-*ayin* verbs. *See* geminate verbs.

doubled by implication. *See* implicit doubling.

double-duty. *adj.* Pertaining to a word, commonly a verb or preposition, that serves two lines of poetic verse but appears only in the first and is implied in the second. *See also* ellipsis.

doublet. *n.* (1) Uses of pairs of abstract nouns that have both a masculine and feminine form. (2) As a technical term in *literary criticism, the repetition of a *type scene in a different line of tradition. Literary critics commonly point to Genesis 12:10-20; 20:1-18; and 26:6-11 as examples of a doublet or triplet.

doubling. *n.* The reduplication of a consonantal sound in a word either for pronunciation, nominal formation or the purposes of verbal inflection; also referred to as gemination, prolongation,* hardening and *reduplication. This is represented in the MT by the diacritical mark known as *dagesh forte.* Joüon §18; MNK §8.2; GKC §12.

doubling *dagesh.* See *dagesh forte.*

doubly closed syllable. *n.* A Semitic syllable that is closed by two consonants (CVCC), which makes up a total of three consonants in the syllable. For example, קָטַלְתְּ is a bisyllabic word formed of an open syllable קָ (CV) and a doubly closed syllable טַלְתְּ (CVCC).

doubly weak verb. *n.* A verb that has a weakness in more than one of the three consonantal positions, such as *pe nun–lamed aleph, pe nun–lamed he, pe yod–lamed he* or *pe yod–lamed aleph.* GKC §76; MNK §18.10. *See also* weak verbs.

double status. *n.* When a noun functions as both the *subject and *object of a sentence. In the Semitic languages this occurs in *reflexive constructions.

dramatic irony. *n.* The use of any information in a narrative, especially concerning the end of the story, that the reader and narrator know but the characters do not. For example, in the comedy of Job, the narrator and reader know God is in control of the situation.

Dt. An abbreviation for *Deuteronomic.

Dtr. An abbreviation for *Deuteronomistic Redactor.

dual number. *n.* A morphological indication of two of a particular nominal. BH and the Semitic languages have three classes of number: singular, plural and dual. The dual is quite rare in BH and is mostly limited to natural body pairs such as the feet or eyes; it is used more liberally in Ugaritic. The BH dual morpheme is ‐ַיִם (e.g., רַגְלַיִם, "feet"). Joüon §91; MNK §24.3; GKC §88; *IBHS* §7.3.

dummy. *See* pleonasm.

durative. *See* linear action.

dyad. *n.* A pair of nouns that are intrinsically related in some way and often found in context together (e.g., male, female).

dynamic equivalence. *n.* A theory of translation that targets a meaning-to-meaning approach rather than a word-for-word equivalence. It takes serious account of not only denotation but also connotation, where a word-for-word literalism may actually carry different connotation in the target language than that of the original.

E

E. An abbreviation for *Elohist. See also* JEDP

Early Northwest Semitic. *n.* A period in the study of the Northwest Semitic family of languages that dates to about 2350-1200 B.C.

East Aramaic. *See* Aramaic.

East Semitic. *n.* The Semitic dialects that are native to Mesopotamia, primarily the area representing ancient Babylon and Assyria.

Eblaite. *n.* The name given to a previously unknown language that was discovered at Tel Mardikh, the site of ancient Ebla in northern Syria.

echo. *See* allusion.

economy. *n.* A style of prose *narrative common to the Hebrew Bible (but not limited to it) that is characterized by terse description and focus on the essentials of the narrative, with only necessary points of background material included.

effected. *n.* An element (usually the object of a transitive verb) that was produced or created by the verbal action. For example, in Gen 1:1: "In the beginning, God created the heavens and the earth," the heavens and earth were produced by means of the verb *create. See also* affected.

Egyptian. *n.* The native language of ancient Egypt in use in various forms from the third millennium B.C. until the fourth century A.D. It was variously represented: first in hieroglyphics and also in hieratic during the imperial periods, then in demotic in the seventh century B.C. until the fourth century A.D., when it was replaced by the Coptic alphabet.

Elamite. *n.* A non-Semitic language (still not well understood) indigenous to southwestern Iran (ancient Mesopotamia) that was represented in *syllabic cuneiform.

elegies. *n.* A poetic genre of *lament in a eulogy-type fashion that is composed on behalf of one who has died. Examples in the Hebrew Bible can be observed in 2 Samuel 1:19-27 for Saul and Jonathan and 3:33-34 for Abner.

elision. *n.* The dropping of a *phoneme. It is common in BH poetry for the purposes of *rhyme or *meter.

ellipse. *n.* A single occurrence of *ellipsis.

ellipsis. *n.* The dropping of a word or *preposition when *context allows. It is common in BH poetry and is often intended for *emphasis by making readers fill in the appropriate word or idea themselves.

Elohist. *n.* The author or the E (Elohistic) source in the *JEDP theory of pentateuchal composition.

Elohistic. *adj.* Pertaining to the Elohist traditions of the Pentateuch in the *JEDP theory.

embedding. *v.* The placement of a sentence or clause within a sentence, such as "He said that *he would go home.*"

emblematic parallelism. *n.* A parallel structure in which a clear statement is made in the first *stiche followed by a *figure of speech in the second.

emendation. *n.* A scribal correction in a manuscript.

emotionals. *n.* A subclass of *impersonals that stress emotions coming upon an entity from an external point of view (e.g., Gen 4:5: וַיִּחַר לְקַיִן מְאֹד, "and it burned toward Cain exceedingly").

emotive. *adj.* Pertaining to anything, especially a literary piece, that displays emotion.

emphatic. *adj.* Relating to any structure or construction used to express emphasis.

emphatic *he*. *n.* The use of the letter ה at the end of a word to express emphasis or as a marker for the *cohortative.

emphatic *lamed*. *n.* The use of the ל preposition as an *emphatic particle in BH. This is also found in other Semitic languages, such as *Arabic and *Akkadian (e.g., Ps 89:19: כִּי (לַ)יהוָה מָגִנֵּנוּ וְ(לִ)קְדוֹשׁ יִשְׂרָאֵל מַלְכֵּנוּ, "for YHWH is our shield, and the Holy One of Israel is our king"). *See also* ethical dative.

emphatic letters. *See* velars.

emphatic state. *n.* Another name for the *articular or *determinative state.

enallage. *n.* The digression in language from strict use of grammatical concord. For example, BH will sometimes use a verb inflected in the masculine with a feminine *subject.

enargeia. *n.* The narration of events as if concurrent with when the narrator tells it.

enclitic. *n.* A grammatical element attached to the end of or following a word. It possesses no *accent of its own but is pronounced as one with the word it follows. *See also* proclitic.

enclitic *mem.* *n.* The rare case of a letter *mem* attached to the end of a word, which is an archaic grammatical form whose function is uncertain.

enclitic pronouns. *See* pronominal suffixes.

encomium. *n.* A generally poetic but sometimes prose literary form that praises the virtues and qualities of a person or thing (e.g., the godly woman in Prov 31:10-31; love in 1 Cor 13).

endocentric expression. *n.* A phrase or word group that has the same syntactical function as its constituent parts; a syntactical construction that should be taken literally, in contrast to an *exocentric expression, which is not to be taken literally.

endophora. *n.* A mother term comprising both *anaphora and *cataphora.

energic mood. *n.* A verbal mood found in some Semitic languages, such as Classical Arabic and Ugaritic. In Ugaritic the mood has two forms and is based upon the prefix conjugation, as also with the Ugaritic *jussive and *subjunctive moods. It is identifiable based upon its likeness to the basic Semitic *prefix conjugations plus the energic *nun,* of which there are remnants in BH as well. Debate has surrounded as to whether it is a volitive mood or not.

energic *nun.* *See* paragogic *nun.*

enumeratio. *See* merismus.

environmentals. *n.* *Impersonal verbs that describe environmental conditions (e.g., Ps 68:14 [MT 15]: תַּשְׁלֵג בְּצַלְמוֹן, "It was snowing in Zalmon").

epanaphora. *See* anaphora.

epenthesis. *See* anaptyxis.

epenthetic *nun.* *See* paragogic *nun.*

epexegetical. *adj.* Pertaining to any grammatical construction or *particle that points out, brings attention to or makes a statement in regard to something else. *See also* epexegetical genitive.

epexegetical genitive. *n.* A genitive with the force of "concerning" or ' regarding." For example, עַם־קְשֵׁה־עֹרֶף, "a people stiff-of-neck" (Ex 32:9), is best understood as "a people who are stiff—regarding their necks," implying stubbornness.

Ephraimite. *n.* A subdialect of Hebrew (for which there is evidence in the Hebrew Bible) spoken in *Transjordan by the Ephraimite tribe.

epic. *n.* A literary genre observed in classical literature that is characterized by a long story of a heroic figure made up of multiple scenes and sometimes poetic rhythm. Ancient Near Eastern examples of epic include the Babylonian Gilgamesh Epic, the Ugaritic Baal Cycle and the biblical book of Job. Some would also include as examples such stories as the David and Elijah cycles in Samuel and Kings.

epicene nouns. *n.* A class of nouns in which both masculine and feminine entities are identified by one form. In BH these are usually animals, such as אַלּוּף, "ox," and זְאֵב, "wolf."

epicoena. See epicene nouns.

epiglottal. *adj.* Relating to a phoneme articulated with the epiglottis, the flap of cartilage at the back of the throat.

epigraphic. *adj.* Pertaining to the study of epigraphy or writing on hard surfaces.

epigraphy. *n.* The scientific study of ancient writing surfaces and methods of inscription as well as the inscriptions themselves. The term, taken literally, is concerned with writing upon hard surfaces such as pottery and stone.

epiphora. *n.* Binding verses into a *strophe by using the same word or phrase at the end of each line to thematically link them, such as in the Apocryphal book of Sirach 31:1-2: "anxiety about it drives away sleep . . . and a severe illness carries off sleep" (NRSV). *See also* anaphora.

episode. *n.* In narrative, a discrete story unit that is part of a larger series. In BH, episodes are often marked by a *macrosyntactical device such as וַיְהִי, "and it happened."

episodic. *adj.* Relating to any narrative that is composed of various scenes and stories within the larger story or *epic tale.

epistolary perfect. *n.* The use of a perfective conjugation to announce events that may be present or imminent from the writer's perspective but will be past or completed from the reader's perspective, that is, by the time the recipient receives the correspondence.

epistrophy. *n.* In rhetoric, the repetition of a word or phrase at the end of successive clauses. *See also* epiphora.

eponymy. *n.* A form of *synecdoche in which a name (eponym) of an ancestor is used to refer to an entire nation or location (e.g., the names Jacob and Israel).

ergative. *adj.* Relating to a linguistic system that emphasizes the noun that is most affected by the action of the verb. It is common in Basque and some European languages. BH properly speaking is not ergative, but when using the Niphal it shows some similarities. In such cases, the *direct-object marker אֵת is used with the *subject of a Niphal verb (e.g., Ex 21:28: וְלֹא יֵאָכֵל אֶת־בְּשָׂרוֹ, "its flesh shall not be eaten"). Though proposed by some, the theory of BH ergativity has generally been rejected for its failure to account for the widespread use of the *direct-object marker.

errata. *pl. n.* A list of errors (sing. erratum).

eschatology. *n.* (1) The religious preoccupation with or study of "end times" or of the present age. (2) An ancient Near Eastern literary *genre characterized by vivid imagery and symbolism, prophetic oracles, coming judgment, and the end of the age. Most classify this as *apocalypse, but some prefer to make a narrow distinction between the two. From this point of view, an apocalypse is a translation of history into *allegorical images, and an eschatology is the ecstatic prophetic vision of future events and especially the end of the eon.

Essenes. *n.* An ascetic, quasi-monastic order of Judaism that existed during the New Testament period and is believed by many to have been the source of the Dead Sea Scrolls.

Ethiopic. *See* Geʿez.

ethical dative. *n.* A redundant use of the לְ preposition as an *emphatic particle with a *pronominal suffix; also referred to as the *reflexive or *ingressive use of the *lamed* (e.g., Josh 22:4: וּלְכוּ לָכֶם לְאָהֳלֵיכֶם, "Get [yourselves] to your tents").

ethnica. *See* gentilic.

etiology. *n.* The disciplined study of origins or causation of a particular phenomenon. It essentially answers the question, What gave rise to X?

etymological fallacy. *n.* A common *word-study error that assumes studying the origin of a word will definitively establish its meaning in a particular context and fails to understand *diachronic language growth.

etymology. *n.* The scientific study of word origins and their derivation.

euphemism. *n.* The idiomatic use of a word or phrase in place of another word of phrase that may be offensive or inappropriate.

euphonic. *adj.* Pertaining to smoothness of sound, or *euphony.

euphonic *dagesh forte.* *See dagesh forte* euphonic.

euphonic *ga'ya.* *n.* Use of the *meteg* to distinguish vowel quality. It generally marks a *long *qamets* to differentiate it from *qamets-hatuph.* GKC §16h.

euphonic *nun.* *See* paragogic *nun.*

euphony. *n.* (1) The use of letters or words in a composition for pleasantness of sound. (2) Any change of spelling or *accentuation to produce a more aesthetically pleasing sound in pronunciation.

exceptive. *adj.* Relating to anything that implies an exception or contingency.

exceptive clause. *n.* A *subordinate clause that makes an exception to the *main clause. It is usually introduced by words such as "except" or "unless" and is in general part of a *conditional sentence, such as in Genesis 43:3b: לֹא־תִרְאוּ פָנַי בִּלְתִּי אֲחִיכֶם אִתְּכֶם, "you shall not see my face, *unless your brother is with you!"* Joüon §173; GKC §163.

exclamation. *See* interjection.

exclamatory clause. *n.* A *clause conveying an exclamation or level of heightened emotion, often in the form of a rhetorical question. Joüon §162; GKC §148.

exclusive conjunctions. *See* restrictive particles; exclusive coordination.

exclusive coordination. *n.* Coordination that limits a relationship. BH uses the conjunctions רַק and אַךְ, "only, indeed," or "except that." *See also* inclusive coordination.

execration. *See* imprecation.

exegesis. *n.* The interpretive act of drawing meaning out of a text according to its literary and historical context.

exegete. *n.* An interpreter, primarily of texts; one who conducts *exegesis.

exemplar. *n.* (1) In literary criticism, a person or hero who is held up as worthy of emulation. (2) In text criticism, a manuscript that is used as the standard from which other copies were produced.

exhortation. *See* paraenesis.

existence. *See* particle of existence.

existential clause. *n.* A clause that indicates existence. This is most often expressed by the use of the particle יֵשׁ, which is translated "there is" or "there are." However, it is sometimes expressed by the verb הָיָה (e.g., Gen 18:24: אוּלַי יֵשׁ חֲמִשִּׁים צַדִּיקִם בְּתוֹךְ הָעִיר, "Perhaps *there are* fifty righteous ones in the midst of the city?" Expressions of nonexistence are also put under the classification of existential clauses and are mostly expressed in BH by the particle of nonexistence אַיִן, which is translated "there is not" or "there is no" (e.g., Gen 20:11: רַק אֵין־יִרְאַת אֱלֹהִים בַּמָּקוֹם, "surely *there is no* fear of God in this place").

existential particles. *See* particle of existence; particle of nonexistence.

existential words. *See* particle of existence; particle of nonexistence.

exocentric expression. *See* idiom.

expanded parallelism. *See* synthetic parallelism.

experientials. *n.* A subclass of *impersonal verbs that express an external circumstance coming on an object without stating the subject. *See* emotionals.

expletive. *n.* (1) Technically, words in an expression that are considered *pleonastic elements and add no meaning; (2) profanity and swearing.

explicative. *See* epexegetical.

explicative. *n.* A direct utterance in which the meaning is straightforward and clearly understood; contrast with *implicature.

explicature. *n.* Explicit speech communication.

explosives. *See* plosive.

extant. *n.* An object or feature that is remaining, left over, or that is attested to by a particular discipline such as linguistics or textual criticism. In textual criticism it commonly refers to biblical manuscripts that have survived to this day. In linguistics it may be a grammatical or linguistic feature that was prevalent at an earlier period but fell out of use, though the language still shows vestiges of it in some instances (e.g., *case markers in BH).

extendable letters. *n.* Letters in a Hebrew Bible manuscript that could be stretched or widened in an adorning manner. Manuscript copyists would avoid breaking words and leaving spaces at the end of a line, so certain letters (א, ה, ל, ם, ת) were extendable to provide left justification of columns.

extended parallelism. *See* synthetic parallelism.

extended patterns. *See* vowel patterns.

external plural. *n.* The method of marking nominal numbers by *morphemes that are external to the Semitic root word; contrast with internal plural.

external points. *n.* Supralinear markings that identify a letter or word that should be omitted. Joüon §16h.

extracanonical. *adj.* Relating to books of a religious nature that were not included as part of the official canon, such as the *Apocrypha or *Pseudepigrapha.

extraordinary points. *n.* Masoretic pointing signs indicating that certain letters in a spelling are called into question as doubtful.

extraposition. *n.* (1) A synonym for a *casus pendens.* Some prefer this term because it avoids the use of "case" terminology. (2) A clause modifying a noun that is separated from it by intervening elements such as a predicate (e.g., "The mailman is here, who has your package").

extra-short vowels. *See* compound *shewa.*

F

fable. *n.* A literary *genre in which animals or inanimate objects are portrayed as personalities with human characteristics to teach a moral lesson. Most scholars deny its existence in the Hebrew Bible, although some cite Judges 9:7-21 and 2 Kings 14:9.

factitive. *adj.* Pertaining to a verbal action leading to an end result (e.g., indicative = he is king; factitive = he became king). The term is used in reference to the stems that have been traditionally called intensive, the Semitic D stem (e.g., Ex 28:41: וְקִדַּשְׁתָּ אֹתָם, "and you shall consecrate them"). *See also* Piel; D stem; delocutive.

factitive-passive sequence. *See* active-passive sequence.

family. *n.* In *text criticism, a grouping of *manuscripts that shows evidence of being from the same copyist tradition.

far demonstrative. *n.* A *deictic element that points to distant objects; also referred to as remote demonstratives. BH employs the standard third personal pronouns for its far demonstratives: הוּא and הִיא, "that"; הֵמָּה/הֵם and הֵנָּה/הֵן, "those." Joüon §§36, 143; MNK §36.2; GKC §§34, 136; *IBHS* §17. *See also* near demonstratives.

feet. *See* foot.

field. *See* semantic field.

fientive verb. *n.* A verb that conveys action or a change rather than a state of being; contrast with *stative verb.

figura etymologica. *See* cognate accusative.

figurative language. *n.* The employment of nonliteral language to express a realistic idea. Figurative language may be subdivided into two categories: (1) trope, a singular use such as *metaphor, *simile, *metonymy, *hyperbole and *synecdoche; (2) scheme, a literary form of figurative language such as *allegory, *irony and *parables.

feminine. *adj.* Generally, of any marked nominal or pronominal denoting feminine gender. It must be understood that feminine gender does not directly correspond to the category female, so gender overtones should generally not be sought in morphology.

final *aleph.* *See* lamed-aleph verbs.

final clause. *See* purpose clause.

final guttural. *See* lamed-guttural verbs.

final *he.* *See* lamed-he verbs.

final letters. *n.* The form of certain letters in the square character script of Aramaic and the MT when they appear at the end of a word: ץ-צ, ף-פ, ן-נ, ם-מ, ך-כ. In earlier stages of Aramaic writing, the normal and final forms were not distinguished. With the exception of the letter *mem*, the final form is believed to be the older of the pairs. Joüon §5d; MNK §4.2.

final vowel. *See* characteristic vowel.

finite verb. *n.* A verb that indicates spatiotemporal action and thus receives linguistic marking such as aspect, voice and mood. Such verbs are to be contrasted with nonfinite verbs, which express potential action. *See also* infinitive; participle; volitive moods.

five-syllable (verse). *See qinah* meter.

fixed pairs. *n.* Pairs of words that tend to occur together in poetry and sometimes in prose.

flectional. *adj.* Pertaining to verbal inflection or inflected language in general.

florilegium. Lat. "bundle of flowers." —*n.* An *anthology of sacred or revered texts, such as 4QFlor, which was found among the Dead Sea Scrolls.

focus construction. *n.* A grammatical construction that draws particular focus to a certain part of the sentence, often a *nominative absolute. Focus may also be expressed by word order or a *focus particle. *See also casus pendens.*

focus marker. *See* focus particle.

focus particle. *n.* (1) Any *adverbial element in a clause that draws attention to another word or clause; also referred to as quantifiers because they express general addition or limitation and have an emphatic nuance to them (e.g., Ps 74:16: לְךָ יוֹם אַף־לְךָ לָיְלָה, "Yours is the day, *moreso* yours is the night"). Common examples are אַךְ, "just, only"; אַף, "indeed, also, moreso"; אֶפֶס, "however, only"; גַּם, "also, moreover." (2) More narrowly, a synonym for a *casus pendens.*

folio. *n.* A booklet of four pages formed from one large sheet folded twice in half or a *codex made of the same and bound by sewing the spine.

foot. *n.* Any consistent pattern of grouped syllables with a consistent stress or intonation for producing rhythm and meter in lyric poetry; also called a metrical foot.

foretoned. *n.* A BH word that has the tone syllable on the penultimate syllable. This can cause normally *postpositive accents to be placed in the *prepositive position.

form. *n.* (1) In *form criticism, a *genre; (2) in *linguistics, a *morpheme.

form criticism. *n.* A discipline of critical biblical study of genre classification particularly associated with Hermann Gunkel. He classified biblical literature into two major forms (*prose and *poetry), under which could be found a multiplicity of subgenres. The form-critical method used by Gunkel could be divided into four basic steps: structural analysis, genre classification, determination of setting in life and identification of intention.

form word. *n.* A word whose use is primarily functional and grammatical as opposed to *full words, which have a complete lexical meaning on their own; also known as *particles or *function words. In BH, the *definite article, *relative pronouns, *demonstrative pronouns and the *direct-object marker are all examples of form words. *IBHS* §3.2.2.

formal parallelism. *See* synthetic parallelism.

formations. *n.* The common translation of the traditional Jewish grammatical term בִּנְיָנִים (*binyanim*), which refers to the vowel *stems of Hebrew. *See also* derived conjugations.

formative. *See* afformative.

formative letters. *n.* Letters used with a root word in the formation of a noun in Semitic dialects. Early BH grammarians further distinguished between the *forma nudae*, nouns composed of only the base root letters, and the *forma actuae*, nouns using these extra formative letters.

Former Prophets. *n.* The subsection of the *Nebiim division of the Hebrew *canon that comprises the historical books: Joshua, Judges, 1 and 2 Samuel, 1 and 2 Kings. *See also* *Latter Prophets.

Formgeschichte. *n.* The German term for form criticism.

Fragmentary Targum. *n.* Not really a targum but rather a collection of midrashic comments on the *Palestinian Pentateuch *Targum; also known as *Targum Jerusalem II.*

free. *adj.* Denoting any grammatical, morphological or syntactical unit that may stand alone; contrast with *bound.

free form. *See* free morpheme.

free inversion. *n.* The ability to break with normal word order without changing meaning, as in the case of *fronting. This stands in contrast to English, where word order partially defines word function.

free morpheme. *n.* A single *morpheme that may stand alone in communication; contrast with *bound morphemes.

free variation. *See* variation.

frequency. *n.* The frequency with which a word is used in a language.

frequentive action. *See* iterative.

fricative. *n.* A *phoneme that is pronounced by a narrowness in the air passage, which causes friction as the air passes through. The English letters *f* and *v* and the Hebrew letters ב and פ, when aspirated, are considered *fricative continuants.

fricative continuant. *n.* A *phoneme characterized by both the narrowed air passage of a fricative and the characteristic continuing unbroken airflow of a continuant, such as English *f* or *ph*. *See also* fricative; continuant.

front vowel. *n.* Any vowel quality pronounced near the front of the mouth, such as long *e*, short *e* and short *i*. *See also* back vowel; rounded vowel.

fronting, fronted. *See* free inversion.

fulcra. *See matres lectionis.*

full vowels. *n.* Any vowel in the masoretic vowel pointing system that has full pronunciation (e.g. *patach, qamets, seghol, tsere, hireq, holem*). They may be contrasted with *half-vowels, which have a hurried pronunciation. Any consonant with a full vowel comprises a stand-alone syllable; a consonant with a half vowel does not comprise an independent syllable.

full word. *n.* A word having intrinsic lexical meaning, such as a noun, verb, adjective or adverb; contrast with *form word.

full writing. *n.* The spelling of BH words in the MT through the use of *matres lectionis;* traditionally known as *scriptio plene*. *See also* defective writing.

function word. *See* form word.

furtive *patach.* *n.* A helping vowel or *glide placed under a hard guttural letter after an accented long vowel. This is the only case in BH where two vowels are pronounced consecutively and a vowel in Hebrew is pronounced before the consonant it stands below (e.g., רוּחַ, "spirit, wind," is pronounced ru-ach, not ru-cha). *See also* gutturals.

future. *n.* The expression of a potential or forthcoming action; e.g., "he will speak." Expressed primarily in BH by the *prefix conjugation.

futurum instans. *n.* A future expression (common in Eng.) where the future is used to describe an immediately future action with a high level of immanency: e.g., "I am going to the market."

G

G stem. *See* Qal.

gapping. *See* ellipsis.

Gattung. Germ. "type." —*n.* A literary term for *genre.

Gattungforschung. *See* genre criticism.

Gattungsgeschichte. *See* genre criticism.

gaʿya. *See* meteg.

Geʿez. *n.* The language of the Semitic colonists of Abyssinia who were converted to Christianity by Coptic missionaries in the fourth century A.D.; also known as South Arabic, Amharic, Abyssinian or Ethiopic. A translation of the Bible was produced in this language, and although it ceased being spoken in about the fourteenth century of the common era, it remains in use as a literary or canonical language.

geminate. *n.* A doubled consonant or a verb with a doubled consonant.

geminate verbs. *n.* Weak verbs with identical second- and third-position consonants in the *triliteral root; also called double-*ayin* verbs. Technically they are *biconsonantal roots that have doubled the final letter to accommodate verbal *inflection (e.g., סבב). Joüon §82; MNK §18.9; GKC §67.

gemination. *See* doubling.

gender. *n.* The formal classification whereby nouns and verbal subjects are grouped so as to indicate syntactical relations. The Semitic languages and BH have three verbal genders (*masculine, *feminine, *common) and two genders (masculine, feminine) for *nominals. Joüon §134; MNK §24.2; GKC §§93-95, 122; *IBHS* §6.

generals. *See* universals.

generative grammar. *n.* A theoretical linguistic discipline developed by Noam Chomsky in the 1950s focusing on language as a system of rules producing or generating sentences and limiting what can and cannot not be a sentence. In this school of thought, a sentence comprises a string, and a language comprises a set of strings.

generics. *See* universals.

Genesis Apocryphon. *n.* An Aramaic targum of Genesis found in Cave 1 at Qumran (abbr. 1Qap Gen[ar]).

genitive. *n.* The grammatical case that expresses genus, origin and possession, most commonly represented in English by the prep. "of," though it can also be loosely expressed by "from." Unlike Greek or Latin, the Semitic languages do not express genitival relationships by case endings but usually by the *construct state and also by *circumlocution. Joüon §§129-130, 139; MNK §§25-26.2; GKC §§127-130; *IBHS* §9.

genitive construct. *See* construct state.

genitive relationship. *See* construct state.

genitive, epexegetical. *See* epexegetical.

Genizah. *n.* A storeroom in an ancient synagogue or scribal center used to store old manuscripts, especially ones being discarded.

genre. *n.* A classification of a written *form that is used in literature as studied in *form criticism. Examples include historical *narrative, *didactic, *prophetic, *apocalypse and the like.

genre criticism. *n.* The critical study of literary forms (*genres) that analyzes the literary patterns, shaping, communicative effectiveness and social conditions (i.e., *Sitz im Leben) in which a form arose.

gentilic. *n.* A Semitic adjectival *sufformative that indicates an ethnic or national class of people. For example, BH employs the gentilic *yod* (e.g., מוֹאָב, "Moab"; מוֹאָבִי, "Moabite").

gentilic yod. *See* gentilic.

gerund. *n.* In English, a verbal noun that is marked by -*ing* (though not all words using -*ing* are gerunds) and that is only used as a noun: (e.g., "walking" is fun). In BH, the infinitive construct may sometimes be translated as a gerund (e.g., "to praise God is good" = "praising God is good"), but the parallel between the BH infinitive construct and the English gerund is not identical.

gerundive. *adj.* Grammatically, denoting potentiality. *See* gerund.

Geschichte. *n.* A German term for history.

glide. *n.* A *phoneme that is considered to be a transitional sound. Glides are neither *plosives nor *continuants. They are considered semivowels in that their pronunciation always leads into a vowel sound, and they usually cannot stand alone. They may be combined with a regular vowel to form a *diphthong. The English letters *y* and *w* and the BH letters י and ו are voiced glides. *See also* furtive *patach*.

global aspect. *n.* The use of an *iterative or *durative *perfective in order to convey a summarizing of repeated or continuous past events. Joüon §111e.

gloss. *n.* A parenthetical comment for contextual clarification or explanation within or noted to a text. It may be the work of either an author or an editor.

glottal stop. *n.* Any consonantal sound that is formed in the back of the throat whereby the glottis is momentarily fully restricted. BH examples include א and ע.

gnome. *n.* Any truism or timeless statement of truth.

gnomic. *adj.* Relating to *sapential or proverbial-type language or sayings; any statement of timeless significance.

gnomic perfective. *n.* A use of the *perfective conjugation to convey actions, events, states or ideas that are treated as timeless. This is common in the *sapential writings of the Hebrew Bible and seems to correspond to a present-tense verb in English even though it retains a perfective nuance.

governed element. *See* governing element.

governing element. *n.* A word in a *syntagm that has a ruling function over the other word or words in the chain; traditionally referred to as *regens*. The governing element is contrasted with the governed element (traditionally called *rectum*). It is a fundamental rule of Semitic languages that the governing element usually precedes the governed element. The standard sentence pattern of BH is VSO (verb, subject, object). The verb *(regens)* precedes the subject *(rectum)*, such as in וַיְדַבֵּר מֹשֶׁה, "and Moses spoke." *Prepositions precede the nouns they govern (e.g., עַד הָאִישׁ, "against the man"), and nouns precede *attributive adjectives (e.g., אִישׁ טוֹב, "a good man"). In a *construct chain, the governed element is always the *absolute noun (final position), such as in בֵּית הַמֶּלֶךְ, "the house of the king," or בֵּית דָּוִד, "the house of David."

gradation. *See* vowel gradation.

graded/nongraded. *adj.* Relating to the concept of *comparative degree as applied to *antonymy. A regular binary relation would be tall/short. The concept of comparative (graded) degree makes a contrast relative to another object (e.g., "She is *taller* than her husband").

grammatical agreement. *See* concord.

grammatical ambiguity. *See* ambiguity.

grammatical concord. *See* concord.

grammatical morpheme. *n.* A unit of meaning used with a word to modify its meaning in some way to define *person, *gender, *number, *mood, *case, part of speech or the like. Grammatical morphemes are subclassified into internal, external and syntactical morphemes. External morphemes generally are either prefixes or suffixes, and internal morphemes are infixes, vowel changes and even accents. Syntactical morphemes are *free morphemes (rare in Semitic languages). A large number of Semitic grammatical morphemes are internal (e.g., קֹטֵל, "killing," and קָטַל, "he killed").

grammatical units. *n.* The five basic building blocks of language: *sentences, *clauses, *phrases, *free morphemes and *bound morphemes.

grammatical word. *n.* (1) A word that has a particular meaning, in contrast to a phonological word, which has a particular sound. This distinction can be seen in the past tense of *dream,* which has two forms: *dreamed* and *dreamt.* Both are considered to be the same grammatical word because they have the same function to express a past tense of *dream.* On the other hand, a phonological word such as *can* may be used as a noun (a *can* of soup) or as a verb (he *can* take it). (2) Also may be used as a synonym for *form word.

grapheme. *n.* A sound or concept symbol in a writing system, such as a letter, *logogram or *pictogram.

grave *meteg.* *n.* The use of *meteg to stress a short vowel or an initial *shewa.*

great *ga'ya.* *n.* A *meteg used with long vowels.

Grimm's Law. *See* systematic correspondence.

Grundlage. Germ. "foundation, base." —*n.* A term used by Martin Noth to refer to common penatateuchal traditions behind the J and E sources for the purpose of explaining certain common elements.

Grundstamm. Germ. "ground stem." —*n.* *Base stem.

gutturals. *n.* The letters א, ה, ח, ע and sometimes ר, which behave according to special rules. These letters will always refuse a *dagesh forte and always take a *compound *shewa* rather than a regular *vocal *shewa.* They prefer the *a*-class vowel *patach and often require a phonetic helping vowel called *furtive patach when immediately following an accented full vowel. In theoretical linguistics, the classification of gutturals is further subdivided into

*laryngeals (א, ה) and *pharyngeals (ח, ע). GKC §§22-23; Jouön
§5j-l; MNK §4.

H

habitual action. *See* iterative.

haggadah. *n*. A type of rabbinic *midrash that is based upon nonle-
gal portions of Scripture, such as historical and didactic sections;
also called aggadah. Haggadah is to be contrasted with halakah,
which is formally midrashim based upon the *Torah.

Hagiographa. Gk. "holy writings"; "sacred writings." —*n*. The
third division of the Hebrew Bible, also known as the *Ketubim
(כתובים).

halakah. *See* haggadah.

half-open. *adj*. Pertaining to any syllable with a vocal *shewa*.

half-closed. *adj*. Relating to a single closed syllable that evolved
from what was once two open syllables. For example, originally
the plural "kings" was מְלָכֵי, but over time it became מַלְכֵי. The
two open syllables מְ and לָ became a half-closed syllable מַל. This
takes place when a full vowel becomes a silent *shewa* (properly
called in this case a medial *shewa*). The half-closed syllable is identifiable when preceding a *begatkepat* letter because the letter is not
pointed with a *dagesh lene*, indicating that the preceding syllable is
half-closed.

half-doubling. *See* implicit doubling.

half-vowel. *See hateph* vowel; *See also* full vowel; vocal *shewa*; compound *shewa*.

Hamitic. *See* Hamito-Semitic.

Hamito-Semitic. *adj*. Arcane nomenclature for *Afroasiatic languages.

hand. *n*. *Metonymy for a scribe; in biblical criticism, most often for
an anonymous *author or *redactor of a literary work.

hapax legomenon. Gk. "read once." —*n*. A word that appears once
in a *manuscript. In the MT it is usually marked in the *Masora
Parva by a *lamed* with a dot over its top. Nearly two thousand
words of the approximately eight-thousand-word vocabulary in
the Hebrew Bible are *hapax legomena* (pl. form).

Haphel. *n*. The *Aramaic *causative stem, which is marked by a *he*
*preformative.

haplography. *n.* A manuscript copying error in which lines or words are omitted by reason of similar material in close proximity; contrast with *dittography.

haplology. *n.* The dropping of one or, at times, two syllables in morphology for the sake of smoothing a difficult-to-pronounce morphological combination (e.g., Syr. ʿaryaya becomes ʿarya).

hardening. *n.* The strengthening of a *begadkepat* letter with a *dagesh lene*, the strengthening of a ה with a *mappiq* or the doubling of any consonant by use of a *dagesh forte*. *See also* doubling.

hardening dot. *n.* A *dagesh lene* or a *mappiq*, but sometimes a *dagesh forte*.

harmonization. *n.* A scribal *emendation made during copying for the sake of correcting a seeming inconsistency.

hateph correptum. *See* compound *shewa*.

hateph patach. *See* compound *shewa*.

hateph qamets. *See* compound *shewa*.

hateph segol. *See* compound *shewa*.

hateph vowel. *See* compound *shewa*.

hayah. *n.* The BH word "to be" or "to come to pass" (הָיָה). It is often used in the imperfect with the *waw-*consecutive (וַיְהִי) as a *macrosyntactic element marking a new *discourse.

he demonstrativum. *See* demonstrative *he*.

he directive. *See* locative *he*.

he interrogative. *See* interrogative *he*.

he locale. *See* locative *he*.

he paragogicum. *See* paragogic *he*.

head. *n.* The *governing element of a phrase.

he'amantic. *adj.* Relating to a mnemonic *acronym used by early grammarians for the seven afformative consonants of the BH verbal *morphological system (הָאֵמַנְתִּיךְ).

heavy consonantal suffix. *n.* A *pronominal suffix that constitutes a *closed syllable (CVC). These suffixes may be contrasted with *light consonantal suffixes, which are open syllables (CV) and *vocalic suffixes (V).

Hebrew, inscriptional. *n.* Hebrew from the Iron Age in Palestine that is *extant on hard writing surfaces such as pottery and stone. It does not differ significantly from the BH of the MT, but very little has survived. *See also* Siloam Inscription.

Hebrew language. *n.* An indigenous Canaanite dialect of Syria-Palestine that was adopted by the Israelites and recorded in the Hebrew Bible *canon. Scholars now recognize several major periods in the progression of the language: Classical Hebrew; Mishnaic Hebrew (or Rabbinic Hebrew), which also includes the medieval period; and Modern Hebrew. GKC §2; MNK §§1-3; *IBHS* §1.

heightening. *v.* The raising of a *short vowel to a *long vowel in the *tone syllable.

Heilsgeschichte. Germ. "holy history, redemptive history." —*n.* A method of interpretation associated with German criticism that studies the Bible as a continuous record of God's redemptive work in history.

helping verb. *See* auxiliary verb.

hemistich. *n.* A half-line of poetry; sometimes used as a synonym of *stich or *colon.

hendiadys. *n.* The use of two semantically approximate words together to describe one thing. It is an attempt for one or both to define the other (e.g., Gen 1:2: "and the earth was *formless* and *void*").

Heptateuch. *n.* The first seven books of the Hebrew *canon (Genesis—Judges).

hermeneutics. *n.* Generally, the scientific or disciplined study of interpretation.

hermetic. *adj.* Pertaining to a genre of literature or literary work in which there are dark, secretive and esoteric sayings, ideas and concepts hard to comprehend.

hero. *n.* Often the *protagonist of a story. The hero is usually a person of outstanding skills or virtue who is in some way responsible for bringing the *narrative conflict to *resolution.

heterogeneous. *adj.* Of a different kind. *See also* homogeneous.

heteronym. *n.* Two words with identical spelling but divergent meanings as well as *etymologies (e.g., Heb זָכָר, "male," and זָכַר, "remember"). This is to be distinguished from simple *polysemy, when one word has two distinct meanings.

heterosis. *n.* The use of one grammatical form in the place of another. This is common in the BH use of the *imperative, which takes on various forces, such as *apostrophe or promise or prediction. *IBHS* §34.4c.

Hexapla. *n.* Origen's text-critical manuscript consisting of six parallel columns: BH; BH transliterated into Greek; Aquila; Symmachus; Septuagint; and Theodotion.

Hexaplaric. *adj.* Generally used in reference to a text found among the six columns of Origen's Hexapla; in modern scholarship, of textual corruptions associated with the *Hexapla and thus sometimes with negative connotations.

Hexateuch. *n.* The first six books of the Hebrew canon (Genesis—Joshua.)

Hiphil stem. *n.* The causative active stem in BH. The stem is recognized by its characteristic ה *preformative and its *characteristic vowel *hireq yod (ִ) in its imperfect, *imperative, *infinitive and *participial forms (e.g., יַמְלִיךְ). Other nuances of voice in the Hiphil are the *intransitive causative, *declarative estimative and *concessive. GKC §53; MNK §16.7; *IBHS* §27.1-5. *See also* double accusative.

hireq. *n.* A Hebrew vowel represented by a single dot written beneath the line (ִ) and pronounced as the short-*i* sound, as in "pin." *See also hireq yod.*

hireq compaginis. *See* suffixes of connection.

hireq magnum. *See hireq yod.*

hireq yod. *n.* The plene (*full writing) form of the *i* sound in the masoretic vowel representation system (ִ). It represents the sharp-*i* sound, as in *machine.* See also *hireq.*

Historical Books. *n.* Generally the *Former Prophets subdivision of the *Nebiim in the Hebrew Bible; in reference to the English Bible, usually includes the same plus 1 and 2 Chronicles, Ezra, Nehemiah, Ruth, and Esther.

historical criticism. *n.* The application of modern scientific methods of historical, archaeological and textual investigation to the study of the Bible's origin, composition and the nature of its historical claims.

historical linguistics. *See* diachronic linguistics.

historical perfect. *n.* The use of a *perfective verb for historical *prose *narrative.

Hishtaphel. *n.* A variant of the *Hithpael stem used with a *sibilant in the word-initial position; the last letter of the prefix and the first letter of the root undergo *metathesis. *IBHS* §26.

Hithaphel. *n.* The classification for the *passive/reflexive conjuga-tion of *hollow verbs in BA.

Hithpaal. *n.* A variant *reflexive inflection of the *Hithpael found in the Babylonian tradition of BH. It seems to be a late addition and to have come about under the influence of *Aramaic. It is only found in seven BH verbs. Joüon §52b.

Hithpael stem. *n.* In BH, the *reflexive derivative of the *factitive (BH *Piel). It is formed by adding the reflexive *preformative הִת to the root word and, as in the Piel, the *doubling of the *medial radical. It also possess varied nuances of *voice, like that of the *Niphal, such as *passive and *privative (e.g., הִתְקַדֵּשׁ, "he shall sanctify himself"). Joüon §53; MNK §16.6; GKC §54; *IBHS* §26.

Hithpalel. *n.* A variant of the Hithpael stem. *IBHS* §26.

Hithpalpel. *n.* The inflection of *geminate verbs in a form of the Hithpael stem. The entire diconsonantal root is doubled rather than just the last letter. For example, גל becomes in the perfect third common plural הִתְגַּלְגְּל וּ. *IBHS* §26.

Hithpoel. *n.* Related to the Hithpolel, the proper classification of the passive/reflexive conjugation of *geminate verbs (*double-*ayin* verbs) in BA.

Hithpolal. *n.* A variant of the *Hithpael stem. *IBHS* §26.

Hithpolel. *n.* The grammatical classification of *passive/reflexive formation of hollow verbs in both BH and BA. These are formed on the analogy of BH Hithpael and the BA Hithpeel plus the redu-plication of the final consonant of the biconsonantal root (e.g., קוּם in the Hithpolel is הִתְקוֹמֵם). *IBHS* §26.

Hittite. *n.* An Indo-European language attested in Asia Minor (mod-ern Turkey) that was the language of Hatti, a rival kingdom to Egypt. It is attested in *cuneiform documents from the second mil-lennium B.C., mostly inscribed on clay tablets, and it shows lin-guistic relations to later Attic Greek. Among the outstanding finds are the extant suzerainty and parity *treaties.

Hittite treaties. *See* treaty.

holem. *n.* A Hebrew vowel represented by a single dot written above the line (˙) and pronounced as the *o* sound in the English word *tone*. It is pronounced after the consonant it is above. See also *holem waw*.

holem waw. *n.* The plene (*full writing) form of the *o* sound in the *masoretic vowel pointing system (וֹ). The previous consonantal text represented the *o* sound with the *mater lectionis letter *waw*; the *holem was added later by the *Masoretes. They did not wish to tamper with the present consonantal text, so they retained the *matres lectionis* and added the signs for *holem*. *Holem waw* has the same phonetic value as regular *holem*.

Holiness Code. *n.* A critical designation for Leviticus 17—26 coined by A. Klostermann in 1877. It is characterized by its *paraenetic appeals for morality and ritual purity.

hollow verb. *See ayin-waw, ayin-yod.*

homogeneous. *adj.* Of the same kind. *See also* heterogeneous.

homogeneous letters. *n.* Letters whose sounds are of the same basic nature. This classification is usually based upon common phonetic shifts between dialects (e.g., שׂ-ס; שׁ-ת; ט-צ and ק).

homograph. *n.* Words that are written identically but may be taken as differing words. For example, in English the verb *lead* is different from the noun *lead*.

homoioarcton. *n.* A scribal error caused by similarities in the beginnings of words.

homoioteleuton. *n.* A scribal error caused by similarities in the endings of words.

homonymic clash. *n.* The case when two homonyms may be used in similar contexts and cause an ambiguity in communication.

homonymy. *n.* Two or more words having the same spelling (sign) and pronunciation but different meanings. *Homophones and homonyms should be distinguished in that homonyms have identical spellings while homophones do not (e.g., the word *down* in English may refer to either a spatiotemporal relationship or goose feathers).

homophones. *n.* *Phonemes that sound identical but have different meanings and spellings (e.g., seen and scene; meet and meat). The sounds are identical, but spelling and meaning are divergent.

homorganic letters. *n.* *Phonemes that are pronounced with the same speech organ (e.g., ג, ב, ק).

honorific. *n.* A word used to convey honor and respect toward the *referent. BH commonly employs the honorific plural (*plural of majesty), though honorifics can take on other forms, such as the construct (e.g., Deut 10:17: הוּא אֱלֹהֵי הָאֱלֹהִים וַאֲדֹנֵי הָאֲדֹנִים, "He is *God of gods*, and *Lord of lords*").

Hophal stem. *n.* The *passive causative of the *ground stem in BH. It is built upon the *Hiphil. Joüon §57; MNK §16.8; GKC §53.

hortatory. A term for a *volitive verbal mode.

hymnic. *adj.* Descriptive of songs and poetry.

hyperbation. *See* free inversion.

hyperbole. *n.* An overstatement for emphasis (e.g., Neh 2:3: "I said to the king, *'Let the king live forever'* ").

hypernym. *n.* A word that serves as a general classification for other words (e.g., "tree" is a hypernym for "oak," "pine," "birch," etc.); contrast with *hyponym.

hyponymy. *n.* In semantics, the distinction between general and specific relationships or classes (e.g., "apple" and "orange" are hyponyms of the *superordinate "fruit"); contrast with *hypernym. *See also* co-hyponyms.

I

iamb. *n.* A *metrical foot in which a light initial syllable is followed by a secondary heavy syllable.

iambic. *adj.* Characterized by *iamb.

iambic meter. *See* iamb.

ideogram. *n.* A pictorial representation to convey an abstract idea, as was common in the earliest stages of ancient Near Eastern writing and even today, such as with numerals (e.g., 3). Ideograms are a class of *pictograms.

idiolect. *n.* The use of a language system peculiar to an individual; contrast with *dialect.

idiom. *n.* (1) A language or dialect particular to a certain group of people (e.g., popular idiom); (2) a figure of speech in language expression. Idioms are characteristically nonliteral language whose sense is obscured if they are taken literally (e.g., "I need to *catch a bus!*"). *See also* endocentric expression.

illative. *adj.* (1) A case indicating movement into something; (2) More generally, any construction expressing an inference (e.g., "therefore").

illegitimate totality transfer. *See* totality transfer.

illocutionary. *adj.* With regard to a *speech act, describing a *performative utterance such as an *imperative, *oath or *curse.

imale. Arabic "deflection." —*n.* The tendency of regular *a* to incline toward *ä, e* or *i.*

immediate constituents. *n.* The essential elements that make up a grammatical or syntactical relationship. It is based upon the idea of systematic breakdown of sentential constructions into increasingly smaller units until one reaches *ultimate constituents. For example, in "Young Tommy went home," the immediate constituents are "Young Tommy" (subject) and "went home" (predicate). The ultimate constituents are "Young" and "Tom" "-y," "went" and "home." *See also* ultimate constituents.

imminent connotation. *n.* A discourse implying that an action is expected with a high level of certainty.

immediate demonstratives. *n. See* near demonstrative.

imperative. *n.* The mood of direct command. It is always spoken in the second person (e.g., "You shall X."). In BH the imperative is based upon the *prefix conjugation and formed by dropping the *preformative consonant. BH imperatives cannot be negated but may only express a positive command. Negative commands are expressed via a negative particle with the *jussive. Joüon §§48, 114; MNK §§15.3, 19.4; GKC §§46, 110; *IBHS* §34.4. *See also* volitive moods; cohortative.

imperative sentence. *See* sentence.

imperfect. *n.* A verbal form characterized in BH by *preformative consonants and indicating incompleteness or fluidity of action, with the exception of its use with the *waw-consecutive (in which case it becomes the *narrative tense and thus perfective); also known as the prefix conjugation. There are a variety of possible translations that must be discerned according to *syntax and context, which include *iterativity, *durativity, *future, *present, *present continuous and the like. Joüon §§44, 113; MNK §§15.2, 19.3; GKC §§4, 107; *IBHS* §31. *See also* perfect; waw-consecutive; *wayyiqtol; weqatal.*

imperfective. *adj.* Pertaining to incomplete verbal action or the Semitic prefix conjugations. Such verbs may be translated as present or future action or even as potential action, in the case of the volitive uses of the prefix conjugations. Joüon §§44, 113; MNK §§15.2, 19.3; GKC §§47, 107; *IBHS* §31.

impersonal construction. *n.* A verbal construction with no stated
*agent. *See* impersonals; pleonasm/pleonastic.

impersonal subject. *See* pleonasm.

impersonal verb. *See* impersonals.

impersonals. *n.* Verbs that express an action or state coming upon
an object without a stated subject (e.g., Gen 4:5: וַיִּחַר לְקַיִן מְאֹד,
"and it burned toward Cain exceedingly"; or the common BH discourse initiator וַיְהִי, "and it came to pass"). They are subdivided
into *emotionals, *environmentals and *experientials.

implicature. *n.* The conveyance of an idea without necessarily stating it. For example, "Have you finished mowing the lawn?" implies that there is a lawn to mow.

implicit doubling. *n.* The phenomenon of a BH guttural letter's (ה
or ח) being treated as a doubled letter when appearing in a word-
medial position even it refuses a *dagesh forte*. Because gutturals
are considered "implicitly doubled," they also reject *compensatory lengthening. Joüon §§18b, 20; GKC §20a.

impositive accent. *n.* An accent mark placed on a *tone syllable.
This is to be contrasted with the *conjunctive* and *disjunctive* ac-
cents, which are placed only at the beginning or end of a word.
Joüon §15f. *See also* prepositive; postpositive.

imprecation. *n.* A common genre in ancient Near Eastern literature
characterized by verbal cursing or condemnation of a person,
place, people group, institution or nation.

imprecative, imprecatory. *adj.* Pertaining to imprecation and curse.

improper annexation. *n.* A construct relationship (*annexion) in
which an awkward construction is formed by making a construct
out of an adjective (e.g., Akk. *damqam-inim*, "good of eye").

inanimate pronoun. *n.* A pronoun that points to an inanimate object
(e.g., *what* is used in place of an indefinite object) and should be
contrasted with an *animate pronoun, which points to and identifies *who*. The BH inanimate pronoun is מָה (e.g., Gen 4:10: מֶה עָשִׂיתָ,
"What have you done?"). The generally attested Semitic inanimate
particle is *man*. Joüon §§37, 144; MNK §43.3; GKC §37; *IBHS* §18.2-
3.

inanimate. *n.* A noun having a noncreaturely referent; anything
without personality, such as a rock, tree or palace. Inanimates are
to be contrasted with *animates and *nonanimates (abstracts).

inceptive. *adj.* Pertaining to the beginning of an action or situation.

inchoative. *See* inceptive.

inclusio. *n.* A literary construction in which the *discourse boundaries are marked off by a similar word, clause or phrase. This is often a way of marking a particular theme, such as in Genesis 1:1—2:3, which is marked off by the simple clause בָּרָא אֱלֹהִים, "God created," in the first and last lines, or Psalm 8:1, 10, which is marked off by "Oh LORD, our Lord, how majestic is your name in all the earth!" Inclusio constitutes an extended level of *literary *parallelism.

inclusion. *See* inclusio.

inclusive clause. *n.* A clause marked by an *inclusive conjunction, such as *also*. *See also* inclusive coordination.

inclusive conjunction. *n.* A conjunction that expressess inclusivity (e.g., BH גַּם and אַף, "also"). *See also* inclusive coordination.

inclusive coordination. *n.* A *coordination idea that portrays the objects as being together (e.g., *also* or *both*) rather than in consecutive order. This is primarily expressed in BH by the inclusive conjunctions גַּם and אַף, "also" (e.g., Gen 3:6: וַתִּתֵּן גַּם־לְאִישָׁהּ עִמָּהּ, "and she *also* gave to her husband with her"). The *waw*-conjunctive may also convey inclusivity. *See also* exclusive coordination; disjunctive coordination.

inclusive relations. *See* hyponymy.

incomplete sentence. *n.* A sentence in which an element is omitted and must be understood from context. This omission, known as *ellipsis or *gapping, was previously referred to by traditional grammarians as a *pregnant construction.

indefinite. *n.* In general, not referring to a particular entity; in grammatical terms, pertaining to a noun that does not possess the definite article. Unlike English, BH does not have an indefinite article, so indefiniteness is expressed by the lack of an article and context. *See also* anarthrous; definite; article; articular.

indefinite adjective. *See* predicate adjective.

indefinite numeral adjective. *See* adjective.

indefinite pronoun. *n.* A pronoun that does not point to a specific entity but is generalized (*many, any, anyone, few, some, all, part*).

indefinite subject. *n.* A noun or pronoun that does not have a particular extralinguistic referent. In most cases they are grammatically indefinite. For example, in "Soldiers are trained for combat," the word *soldiers* is used as a theoretical subject and does not point to any soldiers in particular.

independent clause. *See* clause.

independent personal pronoun. *n.* *An anaphoric element that points to a previously stated subject (*antecedent). Independent personal pronouns are *free morphemes and thus can stand alone, in contrast to *dependent personal pronouns (*bound morphemes), which may be used for possessives and *objects.

indeterminacy. *n.* The characteristic of some words, especially abstract nouns, to evade clear definition other than subjective opinions.

indeterminate. *n.* A noun that is not determined or that is left undefined (i.e., not made definite). *See also* determinate state.

indicative. *n.* The verbal mood conveying factuality, usually by descriptive speech. In BH it is conveyed by both the *perfect and *imperfect conjugations.

indicative element. *See* deictic element.

indirect accusative. *See* indirect object.

indirect action. *n.* A situation in which the subject commits an action that is mediated either by another person or instrument.

indirect discourse. *n.* A quote in *narrative that is more or less a paraphrase rather than an exact quote; also called indirect quotation. In English, *direct discourse is marked by quotation marks, while indirect discourse is not and conveys the gist of what the speaker said. For example, "He said that he would go to the store" is an example of indirect discourse, which can be contrasted with direct discourse, such as, "He said, 'I will go to the store.' "

indirect object. *n.* A nominal that plays a subordinate and modifying role to the action of the verb; the *substantive that receives the *direct object; also called an indirect accusative or an adverbial accusative (e.g., "He [S] gave [V] the note [DO] to him [IO]"). Joüon §126.

indirect question. *n.* A question that is not spoken or quoted in narrative but rather implied, such as in Genesis 24:21: לָדַעַת הַהִצְלִיחַ יְהוָה דַּרְכּוֹ אִם־לֹא, "in order to know *whether or not* YHWH had prospered his way." In BH it is commonly introduced by the interrogative *he*.

indirect quotation. *See* indirect discourse.

Indo-European. *n.* Describing languages of a similar stock and phylum that are indigenous to Eastern and Western Europe and stretching as far as India. Subclasses of this grouping include Greek, Italic (the Romance languages) Celtic, Germanic, Slavic and the like.

inessive. *adj.* Relating to a nominal construction that conveys an internal location (e.g., "She is *in the car*").

infectum. See imperfect; imperfective.

infinitive. *n.* A verbal noun that may be used in a large variety of ways and is usually marked by the preposition "to." (e.g., "He loves *to run*"). MNK §15.6-7; GKC §45; *IBHS* §§35-36. *See also* infinitive absolute; infinitive construct.

infinitive absolute. *n.* In BH, an infinitive that is recognized primarily by a **holem* or **holem waw* (sometimes by a *tsere*) as a **characteristic vowel and is most commonly used for emphatic constructions with a **cognate finite verb (e.g., Gen 2:17: מוֹת תָּמוּת, "you shall most definitely die"; lit., "dying you shall die"). An infinitive absolute can also stand by itself, but this is more rare. Joüon §§49, 123; MNK §§15.7, 20.2; GKC §§45, 113; *IBHS* §35.

infinitive construct. *n.* In BH, an infinitive that is most commonly found with the לְ preposition, though it may also take other **inseparable prepositions or even stand alone, and that usually conveys the same idea as the English infinitive "to X" (e.g., לִשְׁמֹר, "to keep"). The infinitive construct may stand in all syntactical positions and may have both a **subject and an **object. The infinitive construct may take **pronominal suffixes, which can also act as either a subject or an object of the infinitive. Joüon §§49, 124; MNK §§15.6, 20.1; GKC §§45, 114; *IBHS* §36.

infinitive phrase. *n.* A phrase with an **infinitive acting as the governing element (e.g., "He went outside *to walk the dog*").

infix. A **bound morpheme inserted into a word for **morphological purposes, such as **doubling the **medial consonant in the **Piel stem. *See also* prefix; suffix.

inflection. *n.* (1) The morphological modification of a word's meaning by the use of various **afformatives; (2) the systematic organization of a verb's morphological spectrum according to **person, gender, **number and so forth. Joüon §§95-97.

inflectional language. *n.* A language that possesses a system of *morphological inflection for the purpose of word formation. Greek and Latin are examples of inflectional languages. *See also* agglutinative; polysynthetic language; isolating language.

inflectional morphology. *See* morphology.

informative. *See* infix.

ingressive. *adj.* Pertaining to a quasi-*stative verb that describes not merely a state but the creation of one. Ingressive verbs may be called verbs of becoming (e.g., "He grew weary from the journey"; or, "She became a confidant to him"). In BH, the ingressive-stative is often communicated by use of the *Niphal stem, but some verbs have an inherent ingressive nuance.

initial *aleph.* *See* pe-aleph.

initial guttural. *See* pe-guttural.

initial *nun.* *See* pe-nun.

initial *waw,* **initial** *yod.* *See* pe-waw, pe-yod.

innovation. *n.* Changes in a language, especially those that are different from the typical pattern of a particular family or class of language dialects. *See also* conservatism.

inscription. *n.* Writing carved or inscribed on any hard surface, especially stone and pottery.

inscriptional Hebrew. *See* Hebrew, inscriptional.

inseparable preposition. *n.* In BH, a preposition that must be prefixed to a nominal, infinitive construct, or pronominal suffix (בְ, לְ, כְ). Inseparable prepositions are *bound morphemes and are pointed with a vocal *shewa*, except when they are used with the *definite article. In this case, the ה is dropped, and the preposition adopts the pointing of the article. *See also* separable preposition.

inseparable pronouns. *See* pronominal suffixes.

instrumental. *adj.* Denoting instrumentality, that is, the means by which an action was committed. In the Semitic languages, instrumentality is expressed by prefixes and context (e.g., Josh 11:10: וַיָּשָׁב יְהוֹשֻׁעַ בָּעֵת הַהִיא וַיִּלְכֹּד אֶת־חָצוֹר וְאֶת־מַלְכָּהּ הִכָּה בֶחָרֶב "And Joshua returned at that time and captured Hazor and her king and struck them *with the sword*").

integration. *See* borrowing.

intensive. *adj.* Relating to any morphological or syntactical structure that conveys an intensification of the action.

intensive active. *n.* A less-accepted term in recent scholarship for the Semitic D stem (*factitive active), which is characterized by the *doubling of the *medial consonant (e.g., BH *Piel stem: קִטֵּל).

intensive passive. *n.* A less-accepted term in recent scholarship for the Semitic Dp stem (*factitive passive*), which is characterized by the *doubling of the *medial consonant and an *a*-class theme vowel (BH *Pual stem: קֻטַּל).

intensive plural. *See* honorific.

intentional fallacy. *n.* The attempt to read behind the text in order to discover the author's intentions in writing.

interchange (consonantal). *n.* The replacement of one consonant by another, most often for the sake of smooth pronunciation.

interdental. *n.* An aspirated *dental *continuant, such as ת in BH and the θ in Koine Greek, which are pronounced as English *th*.

interference. *n.* The clash of two or more *dialects in a geographical location. *See also* bilingualism; loanword; borrowing.

interjection. *n.* A word or utterance that expresses an exclamation or strong feeling and engenders surprise to the hearers. It is often grammatically separate from the following sentence (e.g., BH הִנֵּה, "Behold!" or "Alas!").

interlingua. *See* lingua franca.

internal accusative. *See* cognate accusative.

internal adjunct. *n.* An adverbial composed of an adjective that is employed to modify the force of a verbal idea.

internal object. *See* cognate accusative.

internal passives. *n.* Semitic *conjugations that express passivity by vowel changes and function as passive conjugations (Pual, Hophal). They are to be contrasted to the Niphal and Hithpael, which express passivity secondarily. Joüon §55.

internal plural. *n.* The method of marking the number of a Semitic root word by the insertion of an internal vowel pattern. Contrast with *external plural.

interpolation. *n.* The later insertion of nonoriginal material into a *manuscript.

interrogative. *adj.* Pertaining to a question.

interrogative adverb. *See* interrogative particle.

interrogative clause. *n.* A complete thought expressing a question or request. GKC §150. *See also* clause.

interrogative *he*. *n.* In BH, a prefixed letter ה pointed with a *hateph* *patach* (דַ) used to introduce and mark a simple question. Joüon §102i; MNK §§11.8, 43; GKC §150c-d.

interrogative particle. *n.* An *adverbial *particle that introduces a question. BH has a number of interrogative particles, such as the *animate pronoun מִי, "who," and the *inanimate pronoun מָה, "what." They ask who, what, when, where or how. Joüon §§37, 102i, 144; MNK §§36.4, 43; GKC §37; *IBHS* §18. *See also* interrogative *he.*

interrogative pronoun. *See* interrogative particle.

interrogative sentence. *n.* A sentence or clause that forms a question. Joüon §161; GKC §150. *See also* interrogative particle.

intertextual. *adj.* Pertaining to the internal thematic relations among separate texts, especially canonical texts.

intervocalic. *n.* A consonant inserted between two vowels.

intonation. *n.* The natural tendency to produce certain tonal patterns for certain kinds of communication, such as the difference between a *declarative statement and an *interrogative.

intransitive verb. *n.* A verb that does not take a *direct object; usually a *stative verb (e.g., "The boy *grows*"). *See also* transitive verb; stative verb.

introverted parallelism. *See* chiastic sentence.

invective. *See* imprecation.

inversion. *See* free inversion.

inversive. *See* wayyiqtol; weqatal.

inverted *nun*. *n.* An upside-down *nun* that occurs nine times in the MT. Its symbolic purpose is highly disputed among textual critics.

inverted parallelism. *See* chiastic sentence.

inverted tenses. *See* wayyiqtol; weqatal.

ipsissima verba. Lat. "the very words." —*n.* Technical terminology referring to a statement as being the exact words of the author or the person being quoted.

ipsissima vox. Lat. "the very voice" —*n.* Used narrowly, a very close but not exact quotation. It is also used synonymously to *ipsissima verba* referring to a quotation with the exact words.

irony. *n.* (1) A statement that in context could only realistically mean the opposite of what is actually said; also called *litotes. For example, one might say "great job" to someone who wrecked a car, which sarcastically implies that the action was not great at all. (2)

In literature, a sequence of events having an outcome contrary to what was expected. A classic example of literary irony in the Hebrew Bible is in the book of Esther, in which Haman is hung upon the gallows that he had constructed for hanging Mordecai.

irreal conditions. *See* unreal conditions.

irreal moods. *See* volitive moods.

irrealis. *See* unreal conditions.

irregular verbs. *See* weak verbs.

Isaiah Scroll. *n.* Most often referred to as the "Great Isaiah Scroll," one of the most well-preserved manuscripts from the Dead Sea Scroll library discovered at *Khirbet Qumran.

isogloss. *n.* The demarcation between respective language dialects. These points of demarcation may be as subtle as the pronunciation of a consonant.

isolating language. *n.* A language that tends toward word separation and shorter words. Such languages usually require several words to express a complete thought, unlike *agglutinatives, which may express a complete thought by one complex word, or a *polysynthetic language, which may even express even longer constructions. English is an example of an isolating language. *See also* agglutinative; polysynthetic language; inflectional language.

isomorphic. *adj.* Having the same structure as something else. In linguistics, the term refers to language systems that have a similar structure in their respective morphological systems (e.g., the Semitic languages).

iterative. *adj.* Characterized by an action that is habitually repeated. This is also called frequentive, habitual or customary action. In BH this may be expressed by the use of the *yiqtol or the *weqatal. GKC §§107, 112.

iterative adverb. *n.* A type of numeric representation that expresses how many times an action took place (e.g., once, twice, three times, four times). *See also* numerals.

Ithpaal. *n.* The *aleph*-preformative form of the passive/reflexive conjugation in BA. It is formed by use of the *aleph-tav* preformative rather than the usual *he-tav*. *See also* Hithpaal.

Ithpeel. *n.* The *aleph*-preformative form of the passive/reflexive conjugation in BA. It is formed by use of the *aleph-tav* preformative rather than the usual *he-tav* preformative. *See also* Hithpeel.

Ithpoel. *n.* The Ithpaal conjugation of geminate verbs in BA. *See also* Hithpoel.

itture sopherim. עטורי ספרים, "scribal omissions." —*n.* The purposeful leaving out of certain elements in the Hebrew Bible by ancient Jewish textual scholars.

J

J. Abbreviation for the German *Jahwist* (Eng. Yahwist). *See also* JEDP

Jahwist. *n.* The proposed author of the J (Jahwistic) traditions of the Pentateuch. *See also* JEDP theory.

Jahwistic. *adj.* Pertaining to the author or source designated Jahwist in the *JEDP theory of pentateuchal composition.

Jamnia. *n.* A Location in Palestine (also known as Yavneh) of a supposed rabbinic council held in the late first century for the standardization of the Hebrew Bible that would be the predecessor of the MT. Some scholars deny that it was a council at all in favor that it represented a major rabbinic academy.

JEDP theory. *n.* The Documentary Hypothesis, which purports that the Pentateuch is the collation of four source documents: J for Yahwist (Germ. Jahwist); E for Elohist; D for Deuteronomist, and P for the Priestly source. This theory was popularized by K. H. Graf and Julius Wellhausen and developed further by Martin Noth and others.

Judeo-German. *See* Yiddish.

jussive. *n.* A *volitive mood of BH and Semitic languages that is based on the *prefix conjugation. In *strong verbs, its form is identical to the regular prefix conjugation form and thus must be identified according to context. In weak verbs, the root will undergo a shortening referred to as *apocopation: the dropping of a *word-final *guttural letter (most often ה). The jussive conveys a wish, permission or an indirect command in the second and third persons (e.g., Gen 1:3: אוֹר יְהִי, "let there be light"). Like *cohortatives, jussives are often accompanied by the emphatic particle נָא. Joüon §§46, 114; MNK §§15.5, 19.4; GKC §§48, 109; *IBHS* §34.3.

juxtaposition. *n.* The syntactical placement of *free morphemes side by side to form a grammatical relationship, often for creating an *appositive or *genitive relationship.

K

kal. See Qal stem.

kaph veritatis. n. The *kaph* preposition when it is employed pleonastically. *See also* pleonasm.

kamnephets letters. n. Hebrew letters that have a final form; also spelled *kemnephatz*. The word is formed from an *acrostic of the five BH/BA letters with final forms: כ-ך, מ-ם, נ-ן, פ-ף, צ-ץ. *See also* final letters.

kernel. n. A linguistic term that refers to the several basic sentence construction patterns in a language as proposed by Noam Chomsky in his theory of *transformational grammar. A kernel sentence is the basic sentence upon which all *modifiers, *adjectives, *adverbs, *clauses and *phrases are attached for the purpose of further clarifying the meaning of the kernel sentence. For example, "The old man rode the red double-decker bus to his home" could be reduced to the kernel "the man rode to his home" or even further to the kernel "man rode."

kernel analysis. n. A form of sentence analysis that seeks to drop all *modifiers in order to reduce a sentence to its basic, *kernel form. According to Peter Cotterell and Max Turner, the discipline of kernel analysis is based on the assumptions that complex sentences are built on simple ones, and the reduction of a complex sentence to its kernel will most clearly state what is being affirmed.

kethebh. See Kethib.

Kethib. n. "what is written." —n. Words in the MT that are written in the text but doubted or rejected by medieval rabbinic textual scholars in regard to their authenticity. They were retained out of reverence for the text and were thus noted in footnotes with replacement words known as *Qere, which was to be used during public readings. Joüon §16e; MNK §9.7; GKC §17.

Ketubim. BH כתובים, "writings." —n. One of the three traditional divisions of the Hebrew canon, namely, the Torah (Law), Nebiim (Prophets) and Ketubim (Writings). The Writings consist of Psalms, Job, Proverbs, Ruth, Song of Songs, Qoheleth (Ecclesiastes), Lamentations, Esther, Daniel, Ezra, Nehemiah, and 1 and 2 Chronicles. *See also* Tanak.

Khirbet Qumran. See Qumran.

Klage. See lament.

L

labial. *n.* A letter pronounced with the lips (labia), such as ב and פ. *See also* bilabial; labiodental.

labiodental. *n.* A *fricative letter pronounced via the pressing of the lower lip against the top teeth, as with English phonemes *v* and *f;* also called labiodental fricative. *See also* bilabial.

Lachish letters. *n.* A collection of inscriptional correspondences on potsherds between military personnel just before the fall of Lachish to Nebuchadnezzar in 589 B.C.; also referred to as the Lachish *ostraca. They offer epigraphic and historical data to aid in our reconstruction of the fall and exile of Judah to the Babylonians.

lacuna. Lat. "hole." —*n.* In textual criticism, a gap or lost section of a text or manuscript. Causes of lacunae may be accidental or purposeful, from a damaged manuscript to intentional scribal alteration.

***lamed-aleph* verbs.** *n.* Weak verbs that are characterized by the presence of an א in the *word-final position of the *triliteral root and that exhibit unique inflectional patterns because of this weakness; also called III-*aleph* or final-*aleph* verbs (e.g., מצא). Joüon §78; MNK §18.4; GKC §74. *See also* weak verbs.

lamed auctoris. *n.* The use of the prefixed preposition ל to ascribe authorship, as commonly found in the Psalms. It has also been debated that these uses could indicate the dedication of the psalm to the person (e.g., Ps. 50: מִזְמוֹר לְאָסָף, "A psalm of Asaph" or "A psalm for Asaph").

***lamed*-guttural verbs.** *n.* Weak verbs with a guttural letter in the *word-final position of the *triliteral root; also called III-guttural verbs or final gutturals. These include both the final-*aleph* and final-*he* verbs. GKC §65. *See also* weak verbs.

***lamed-he* verbs.** *n.* Weak verbs that have a letter ה in the *word-final position of the *triliteral root; also called III-*he* verbs. Joüon §79; MNK §18.5; GKC §75. See also *weak verbs.*

***lamed* of advantage.** *See lamed* of interest.

***lamed* of disadvantage.** *See lamed* of interest.

***lamed* of interest.** *n.* The use of the inseparable preposition ל with pronouns or nouns in order to denote circumstances that concern the referent (e.g., Gen 21:17: מַה־לָּךְ הָגָר, "What *concerns* you, Hagar?" or "What is wrong with you, Hagar?").

lament. *n.* A *form-critical technical term for a genre of poetic writing characterized by sorrow, anger and fear, such as the book of Lamentations.

lamentation verse. *See qinah* meter.

langue. Fr. "language" —*n.* A term coined by Ferdinand de Saussure to refer to a language system as a binding force upon people's communication. This is to be distinguished from **parole*, which is a particular system as employed by an individual (i.e., the actual utterances).

large letters. *n.* Letters in the MT that were intentionally enlarged in order to mark a text or verse that was of significant import; traditionally called *litterae majusculae*. For example, in Deuteronomy 6:4 of the MT, the *ayin* of the verb שׁמע is enlarged to mark it as the *Shema.

laryngeal. *n.* A guttural letter that is pronounced by a slight restriction of the larynx (e.g., א and ה). The category represents a more gently pronounced subclassification of guttural letters, as compared with *pharyngeals.

Late Biblical Hebrew. *n.* The BH attested in documents from the postexilic period of Israel's history and that bears close affinity to the Hebrew represented in the Dead Sea *manuscripts. MNK §2.1. *See also* Classical Biblical Hebrew.

lateral. *See* lateral continuant.

lateral continuant. *n.* A type of *continuant that is pronounced by pressing the tongue against the upper gums behind the top front teeth (alveoli) with the sides of the tongue not touching. As the air is forced through, it travels over the sides of the tongue, continuing under it and out the mouth, resulting in an *l* sound. As with any other continuant, the airflow is theoretically unbroken. The only lateral continuant in BH and BA is the *lamed* (ל).

Latter Prophets. *n.* A subsection of the *Nebiim division of the Hebrew canon consisting of the prophetic books proper (Isaiah, Jeremiah, Ezekiel, etc.); contrast with *Former Prophets, which comprise the *Historical Books.

lead word. *n.* Generally, the first word in a grammatically constructed phrase. The term is often used for the first word in an appositional phrase; also called a head. The first word is the lead word, and the second constitutes the *appositive. The term may also be used for the *governing element of a construct or any other grammatical relationship.

lectio difficilior. Lat. "difficult reading." —*n.* In text-critical studies, the more grammatically difficult of two or more *variant readings. A principle of text criticism that assumes the harder reading is the more "authentic," assuming that a smoother reading was the work of a later scribal *redaction.

leitmotif, leitmotiv. See motif.

lengthening. *See* compensatory lengthening.

Leningradensis, Codex. *n.* An important Hebrew Bible manuscript for text criticism dating to approximately A.D. 1008 and the central text for most modern Hebrew Bible editions.

leveling. *See* smoothing.

lexeme. *n.* A word in its simplest dictionary form; an independent element of semantic content (meaning), in contrast to *bound morphemes, which provide semantic content but are dependent and must be attached to a lexeme; also called a semanteme. *See also* lexical morpheme.

lexical. *adj.* Pertaining to word meaning or the lexicon of a given language.

lexical ambiguity. *See* ambiguity.

lexical field. *See* semantic field.

lexical form. *See* lexical morpheme.

lexical morpheme. *n.* The particular form of a word chosen by lexicographers that exhibits the most fundamental meaning(s) of a word. For example, BH verbs are generally always listed in the *Qal third masculine singular form, unless there is no Qal form, then usually the *infinitive construct.

lexical semantics. *n.* The study of word meanings; the study of a word's *semantic field, including all possible meanings it may assume.

lexicography. *See* lexical semantics; lexicology; etymology.

lexicology. *n.* The discipline of developing reliable methods of *word study.

light consonantal suffix. *n.* A *pronominal suffix that begins with a consonant and ends with a vowel, thus constituting an open syllable (CV). *See also* heavy consonantal suffix; vocalic sufformative.

light *waw*. *See* *waw*-conjunctive.

limiting adjective. *See* adjective.

line. *See* stich.

linear action. *n.* Used with a verb, continuous action. In BH this may be expressed by the imperfect *(yiqtol)* or by the perfect with the *waw*-consecutive *(weqatal)*. GKC §§107, 112. *See also* iterative.

lingua franca. *n.* A common secondary tongue used by people of differing ethnic and language backgrounds for communication; a trade and commerce language. Aramaic and then Greek were each the *lingua franca* of their day that many nations used for trade and diplomacy.

linguals. *n.* Phonemes produced by one or more vibrations of the tongue, such as ל and ר. Joüon §5n.

linguistic factitive. *See* delocutive.

linguistics. *n.* The scientific study of language expression and language systems. The term is generally applied to the discipline of descriptive linguistics, as contrasted with prescriptive linguistics, also known as *classical grammar. Though similar, they are to be clearly distinguished according to method and intent. While classical grammar establishes rules and makes judgments on correct and incorrect grammar, modern linguistics does not wish to make value judgments about correctness (the so-called *classical fallacy) but rather evaluates an utterance upon the merit of its power to communicate effectively. Theoretical linguistics is subdivided into four subdisciplines: *phonology, *morphology, *syntax and *semantics.

linking condition. *n.* A morphological condition used to bind *morphemes together. For example, in BH, the third-person feminine perfect *morpheme (הָ) is linked by the reduction of the last vowel of the masculine form to a silent *shewa* (שָׁמְרָה = הָ + שָׁמַר) This may also be done by the use of a *linking vowel or by *proclisis (the loss of accentuation). The linking by loss of accentuation is common in BH with the use of the separable prepositions, and this is most often marked by the use of a *maqqeph in the MT (e.g., Gen 13:3: עַד־הַמָּקוֹם, "unto the place"). The preposition "unto" has no accent of its own and is pronounced together with the following word. Instead of ʿad hammāqôm, it is pronounced ʿadhammāqôm. *See also* proclitic; enclitic.

linking vowel. *n.* A vowel that creates a *linking condition for

*bound morphemes. Joüon §61d.

liquid. *n.* A class of *phonemes that produces a roll of the tongue when pronounced, such as the letters *r* and *l* (BH ר and ל).

literary criticism. *n.* Broadly, an umbrella term for the various approaches to biblical literature. Used generally, the term refers to higher criticism of the Bible; more narrowly and recently, to modern literary approaches to the Bible, including *form criticism.

litotes. *n.* A type of irony; a rhetorical understatement for the sake of emphasizing the opposite of what is literally said, such as saying "You sure don't work very hard, do you?" to a person who *does* work hard. This literary phenomenon is also referred to as both meiosis and *irony.

litterae compaginis. See suffixes of connection.

litterae majusculae. See large letters.

litterae radicales. See triliteral root.

litterae serviles. See formative letters.

litterae suspensae. See suspended letters.

little *gaʿya. n.* The use of *meteg with anything other than a *long vowel.

loanword. *n.* A word borrowed from another language, such as *Aramaisms in the Hebrew Bible, often proper names of places and objects. It is commonly recognized that the BH word for palace (היכל) is actually an adaptation of a more ancient *Sumerian loanword, *egal*.

locative. *n.* The case that expresses location (e.g., "He is waiting *at the train station*"). BH indicates a locative sense by using the *locative *he*, *prepositions and *context.

locative *he. n.* A BH sufformative (ָה) to indicate location or an orientation toward an object. It was previously called by earlier grammarians the *he locale*. It does not affect accent nor receive an accent, and it is thus distinguishable from the feminine ending *he* because of this lack of accentuation. It may even be suffixed to plural endings. MNK §28; GKC §90c-i.

logogram. *n.* Broadly, a letter, symbol or sign that represents an entire word. Logograms were used in the earliest stages of ancient Near Eastern writing. They were not limited to one particular language or dialect but were often pictures of the objects they represented. Consequently, a single document could be read by people of differing languages who could not otherwise communicate. *See also* pictogram.

long imperfect. *See* long *yiqtol*.

long syllable. *n.* In BH, a syllable that is either *closed (CVC) with any vowel or *open (CV) with a *long vowel. Some classify closed syllables with *unchangeably long vowels as *ultra-long syllables. *See also* short syllable.

long verse. *See* qinah meter.

long *yiqtol*. *n.* The *prefix conjugation that expresses *iterative, *customary, *habitual or *distributive actions. These generally break from standard BH narrative word order (VSO) in that it refuses the initial position. See also short *yiqtol*.

lower criticism. *See* textual criticism.

LXX. *See* Septuagint.

M

ma'arik. See *meteg*.

macrocontext. *n.* The larger literary and historical setting of a given *pericope or *utterance.

macrostructure. *n.* The larger mechanical framework of a *pericope or literary work, such as the *acrostic structure of Psalm 119 or the *toledot* structure of Genesis.

macrosyntactic devices. *n.* Syntactical elements that exert influence beyond sentence-level syntax to influence the larger discourse. They function more to relate paragraphs and thoughts rather than to relate sentences. Some in BH function as discourse breaks. The common BH narrative heads וַיְהִי and וְעַתָּה, "now," are used as discourse transitions. MNK §§44.5, 44.6.

main clause. *See* clause.

main field. *n.* The location of a BH clause in which the verb is introduced. It is to be contrasted with the *preverbal field, which refers to all that precedes the verb, most often consisting of the subject and respective modifiers.

mainline. *n.* Variously used to denote the central story line of BH narrative conveyed by use of the *wayyiqtol*, as contrasted to offline background material.

malediction, maledictory. *See* imprecation.

manuscript. A document that was written or copied by hand.

mappiq. n. A hardening dot placed inside the Hebrew letter ה that stands in a *word-final position to give it consonantal value. It should not be confused with the *dagesh lene* or *forte*. Rather, it distinguishes consonantal ה from *mater lectionis* ה. Joüon §11; MNK §9.2; GKC §14. *See also* vowel letters.

maqqeph. מַקֵּף, "binding." —*n.* A horizontal stroke used in the MT to bind two words together in pronunciation. It indicates *proclisis, in which the first word in the series always loses its *accent and they are pronounced as one word. This most often results in vowel reduction and is commonly used to bind the *direct-object marker אֵת to the direct object (e.g., אֶת־קוֹלִי). It may also be used for binding construct nouns. Joüon §13; MNK §9.3; GKC §16.

marked. *See* markedness.

markedness. *adj.* Pertaining to any morphological change in a word from its lexical form, such as the plural *s* being added to a noun (e.g., bug [unmarked] and bugs [marked]). *See also* zero morpheme.

mashal. n. A proverb or proverbial saying in the Hebrew Bible. The term also carries such connotations as a taunt, riddle or byword.

Masorah. Mishnaic Hebrew "tradition." —*n.* The detailed textual notations given in the margins of the MT in the medieval rabbinic period. There were three basic classifications of Masorah in the MT: *masorah magnum, *masorah parvum and *masorah finalis. Masorah magnum refers to the most detailed notations on the MT, which are found in both the top and bottom margins of text. Because of the mass of information it contains, it was published in a separate volume than that of the *BHS*, known as the *Massorah Gedolah*. Masora parva are the notes found in the side margins of the *BHS*. These are written in Aramaic, with some in Hebrew. *Masora finalis* refers to extensive concordance-like material that is found at the end of the MT. Joüon §16; MNK §§8-9.

Masorah finalis. n. (1) Originally, the alphabetical lists taken from the *masorah magna* at the end of the Jacob ben Chayyim Rabbinic Bible; (2) Now, more often (but technically incorrect) in reference to the masoretic statistics found at the end of each book of the Hebrew Bible, consisting of verse count, the center of the book and, in the Pentateuch, the number of *sederim*.

Masora magna. n. The extended commentary and textual notes on the MT that are no longer printed in the margins. These are referenced by the *Masora parva* and are printed in a separate work known as the *Massorah Gedolah*.

Masorah marginalis. *See* Masorah.

Masorah parva. *See* Masorah.

Masoretes. *n.* Medieval Jewish textual scholars who conducted extensive textual analysis of the Hebrew Bible and the Tiberian pointing system.

Masoretic Text. *n.* The text tradition passed down from early rabbinic textual scholars known as the Masoretes (abbr. MT). *See also* ben Asher.

mass noun. *n.* A noun that refers to a corporate body as a singular entity and may not be individually enumerated (e.g., water, people, pepper, forest); contrast with *count noun.

matres lectionis. *See* vowel letters.

medial. *adj.* (1) In Semitic studies, usually a syllable that is *penultimate; (2) the second letter of a *trilateral root.

medial guttural. *See ayin*-guttural.

medial lengthening. *See* doubling.

medial letter. *n.* The middle letter of a triconsonantal root.

medial *shewa*. *n.* A type of *silent shewa* that did not originally mark a *closed syllable but replaced a vowel that eventually dropped out. In such cases, it is now treated as a silent *shewa* and used as a syllable closer. However, if it is followed by a *begadkepat* letter, the *Masoretes would mark the loss of a previous vowel by not using a *dagesh lene. The *begadkepat* letter is then pronounced as a *fricative, not as the expected plosive following a closed syllable. For this reason, these syllables have been referred to as *half-closed syllables. For example, the half-closed syllable with the medial *shewa* is מַלְכֵי, not מַלְכֵּי, which would be fully closed.

medial *waw*, medial *yod*. *See ayin-waw, ayin-yod.*

medial weak verb. *n.* A verbal root that has a weakness in the second (middle) letter of the triconsonantal root. *See also ayin*-guttural; *ayin waw, ayin-yod.*

Medieval Hebrew. *n.* The Hebrew used by rabbinic scholars of the Middle Ages who lived throughout Europe and greater Arabia. While connected to Rabbinic or Mishnaic Hebrew, it must still be distinguished from it.

medioreflexive. *See* Niphal.

Megillah. *n.* Traditional Jewish nomenclature for the book of Esther, but also for any one of the five *Megilloth.

Megilloth. *n.* Five books in the Hebrew canon that are to be read on certain Jewish holidays: Song of Songs, Ruth, Lamentations, Ecclesiastes and Esther.

meiosis. *See* litotes.

***mem* preformative.** *n.* The use of the letter *mem* in the formation of some verbal nouns by prefixing it to the beginning of the word. It occurs in the participles of the derived conjugations in BH and the Semitic languages.

merism. *See* merismus.

merismus. *n.* A poetic technique by which a whole is referred to by either its two major parts or two extremities. Thus, "heavens and earth" refers to the entire cosmos, and "mountains and valleys" refers to the total terrain.

Mesha Stela. *n.* An important monumental inscription found in 1868 composed in Moabite upon a black basalt stone lauding the victory of King Mesha of Moab over Israel. On it are mentioned such important entities as Israel; Omri, the king of Israel, who was King Ahab's father; the men of Gad; and even YHWH.

metalanguage. *n.* The technical language surrounging the study of languages proper.

metanarrative. *n.* Used variously, either elements or ideas outside a narrative or a string of independent narratives together in their historical progression.

metaphor. *n.* A figure of speech in which one thing is described by equating it with another so as to bring out those attributes. For example, "That boy is a fish!" implies that a lad can swim extremely well. *See also* simile.

metaphrase. *n.* An overly literal translation of a text, so literal that the real meaning is often lost; to be contrasted with a *paraphrase.

metaplasm. *n.* Any alteration of a word by the change of a letter, often by metathesis (e.g., BH כבש or כשב for "lamb").

metathesis. *n.* The switching of consonants for the sake of smoothing pronunciation. When the BH *Hithpael stem is applied to a word beginning with a sibilant, the last consonant of the prefix and the first consonant of the root undergo metathesis (e.g., הִת + שָׁמֵר becomes וְהִשְׁתַּמֵּר). Joüon §17b; GKC §19m.

meteg. מֶרֶג, "bridle." —*n.* A *sublinear short perpendicular stroke (usually to the left of a vowel) that acts as a secondary *accent providing a pause in the pronunciation of a *syllable; also spelled *metheg* or *methegh*; also referred to as *maʾarik* ("lengthener") and *gaʿya* ("raising"). It may also indicate the fuller pronunciation of a vowel or syllable. It is also used as a *syllable closer to distinguish the vowels *qamets* and *qamets hatuph*. In such cases it serves to identify an open syllable and indicate that the following *shewa* is vocal. For example, קָטְלָה is pronounced *qa-tela*, not *qot-la*, and מִלְמַעְלָה is pronounced *milmaʿelah*, not *milmoʿlah*. Joüon §14; MNK §9.1; GKC §16.

meter. *n.* The presence of cadence in a composition. It is based upon the periodic reoccurrence of an element, most commonly *accent, but also *syllables and other factors. Within Hebrew Bible studies, the subject is greatly debated. Sometimes the term is used synonymously with *rhythm*, but most scholars today distinguish between them. Currently there are as many as five major schools of thought in regard to Hebrew meter. The traditional school identifies BH meter with accentuation; the semantic-parallelism school finds it within the phenomenon of BH parallelism; the alternating-meter school finds it in the interchange of toned and untoned syllables (this school relies heavily upon masoretic vocalization); the syllabic school finds it in the number and use of syllables. Most focus upon the accented syllables, which are counted to give a cadence number. A verse that has three accented syllables in the first half and three syllables in the second half will be termed a 3 + 3 verse, whereas one with three and two accents will be termed a 3 + 2 verse. The fifth, and probably most prevalent contemporary school of thought, is that BH does not possess meter at all. *See also* iambic; trochaic.

metonymy. *n.* Reference to one significant part of an entity in order to refer to the whole (e.g., "oval office" may be used for the president of the United States or the administration). Metonymy and its close relative *synecdoche are used frequently in the prophetic, apocalyptic and wisdom writings, as well as the Psalms. For example, וְכָל־הָאָרֶץ, "all the land," in Genesis 41:57 is used metonymically to refer to all the inhabitants of the land.

metrical foot. *See* foot.

microcontext. *n.* The immediate historical and literary context of an object of study, usually limited to the *pericope level; contrast with *macrocontext.

microstructure. *n.* The immediate clausal or sentence structure of an *utterance. One may contrast this with *macrostructure, which is the larger utterance construction composed of various sentences.

Middle Assyrian. *n.* An East Semitic language that flourished in northern Mesopotamia (about 1500-1000 B.C.) and was written in *syllabic cuneiform.

Middle Babylonian. *n.* An East Semitic language that flourished in southern Mesopotamia (about 1500-1000 B.C.) and was written in *syllabic cuneiform.

Middle Persian. *See* Persian.

Middle Semitic Languages. *See* Northwest Semitic.

middle voice. *See* reflexive.

midrash. *n.* A type of early rabbinic exegesis characterized by fanciful and whimsical interpretations that generally ignored the literary and historical context of texts. The term may also refer to commentaries written with such methods. *See also* pesher.

milel. מְלְעֵיל. *n.* An accent placed upon the last (ultimate) syllable. *See also* milra.

milra. מְלְרַע. *n.* An accent placed upon the next-to-last (penultimate) syllable. *See also* milel.

mimation. *n.* The tendency of various Semitic languages to employ the letter *m* for various morphological and linguistic uses, including simple smoothing of pronunciation. *See also* nunation.

mimetic. *adj.* Pertaining to literature that contains characters who are intended to be objects of emulation, often with an ethical tone.

min **of comparison.** *See* comparative *min*.

Mishnah. The body of collective rabbinic teachings surrounding the Hebrew Bible attributed to the *Tannaim. The commentaries of the Babylonian and Jerusalem *Talmuds are based upon the Mishnah and the Toseftah.

Mishnaic Hebrew. *n.* The distinct dialect of Hebrew spoken in Palestine from circa 200 B.C. up to roughly about A.D. 400; formerly known as New Hebrew. The term is derived from this dialect's use in the composition of the *Mishnah, *Tosefta and the accompanying commentaries of the Babylonian and Palestinian Talmuds. *See also* Amoraim; Tannaim; Tosefta.

mishqal. Hebrew "weight." —*n.* A phonetic pattern used in the formation of BH nouns. *IBHS* §5.3-7.

mixed stems. *See* weak verbs.

Moabite Stone. *See* Mesha Stela.

mobile *shewa*. *See* vocal *shewa*.

modal aspect. *See* volitive moods.

modal word. *n.* A particle that relates to an entire clause rather than just to a word and thus conveys specific grammatical modes, such as *negation, definiteness or *interjection. The negative particles לֹא and אַל, the definite article הַ, the direct-object marker אֶת, and interjections such as הִנֵּה and הוֹי are all considered to be modal words.

modality. *See* mood; volitive moods.

mode. *See* mood; volitive moods.

Modern Persian. *See* Persian.

modernizing. *n.* A scribal modification to a manuscript or quote in such a way as to reflect the linguistic customs of his own time. It has been observed that the Chronicler, even when quoting from the *Pentateuch, often modifies an older construction to that of his contemporary usage. *See also* archaism; smoothing.

modifier. *n.* A syntactical element that modifies the meaning of another word, such as an adjectival or an adverbial.

monoliteral. *n.* A word or particle composed of a single consonant. *See also* biliteral root; triliteral root.

monophthong. *n.* A single vowel sound produced from two separate vowels.

monophthongization. *n.* The formation of a single vowel sound by the coalescing of two vowels at an earlier stage; to be contrasted with a *diphthong.

monosyllabic. *adj.* Consisting of a single syllable. Monosyllabic words are subdivided into two categories based upon their pluralization: those without *doubling of the final consonant (e.g., שִׁיר is pluralized as שִׁירִים); and those with doubling of the final consonant (e.g., עַם is pluralized as עַמִּים).

mood. *n.* The relation of a verb's action to real time and space; also called mode. The indicative mood implies real action in the spatiotemporal world, while the *volitive moods such as the *imperative, *jussive or *energic all refer to differing aspects of a potential action. GKC §§40, 106-112.

morpheme. *n.* The smallest unit of meaning in a language system. All words are morphemes, but not all morphemes are words. They are subdivided into two categories: *free morphemes, units of meaning (words) that may stand alone; and *bound morphemes, units that must be attached to another word.

morphemic slot. *n.* The set location where a morpheme may be inserted in a word within a language system, such as *prefixes, *suffixes and *infixes.

morphologic pair. *n.* Morphologically related words in parallel lines of BH poetic verse. They do not have to be of the same root, stem or word class, only have some parallel relationship. *See also* morphologic parallelism.

morphologic parallelism. *n.* The patterning of morphological and syntagmatic structures, usually in poetry (e.g., Ps 29:5: "The voice of YHWH breaks [Qal participle of שׁבר] the cedars; YHWH breaks [Piel *wayyiqtol* of שׁבר] the cedars of Lebanon").

morphological conditioning. *n.* A language's breaking with normal patterns because of certain phonological or morphological conditions. For example, the normal plural form for *ball* is *balls*, in contrast to the plural for *man*, which is *men*, not *mans*. *See also* allomorph.

morphology. *n.* The subdiscipline of linguistics that studies word formation. Words are made up of the smallest meaning units (morphemes) that modify the basic lexical meaning as they are attached together. *See also* morpheme.

morphs. *See* allomorphs.

mothers of reading. See *matres lectionis.*

motif. *n.* A theme, idea or image that is developed throughout a literary composition and is often central to the author's communicative intent.

MS. Abbreviation for *manuscript;* MSS is the plural abbreviation for *manuscripts.*

MT. Abbreviation for the Masoretic Text.

multiplicative. *n.* An expression that indicates the multiplication of something, such as twofold, fourfold or a hundredfold (e.g., Gen

26:12: מֵאָה שְׁעָרִים, "a hundredfold"). *See also* distributive.

murmured. *adj.* Referring to a breathy pronunciation, such as of ה or sometimes for a quick and unemphasized vowel sound.

murmured vowel. *n.* In BH, refers to both simple *vocal *shewa* and the *compound *shewa*s.

mutes. *See* plosive.

myth. *n.* Used variously of stories and traditions common in the ancient world usually to explain events with some historical basis, such as creation, religious customs or natural phenomena cast in the framework of very unnatural events or the exploits of the gods. Myths most often sought to provide a tribe or culture with a sense of origin and identity.

N

narrative. *n.* The retelling of a linear succession of events. It generally records a series of events in a chronological order and may be either fictional or historical. BH narrative is characterized by its use of the *wayyiqtol* verbal form.

narrative conflict. *See* conflict.

narrative sequence. *n.* A literary pattern in BH *narrative in which the *waw-relative is used to link a series of verbs in order to convey a consecutive relationship to the events. It represents the basic form of BH historical narration.

narrative tense. *n.* (1) A broad classification of anything that may be used in the expression of historical narrative; (2) in BH, the *wayyiqtol* conjugation; (3) certain uses of the participle in BA. The narrative tense is used for expressing the narration of past events.

narratology. *n.* The formal study of narrative texts, especially in regard to their structure.

narrow qamets. *See* qamets hatuph.

nasal. *See* nasal continuant.

nasal continuant. *n.* A letter pronounced by opening the velum and allowing the air to flow out the nostrils rather than the mouth, such as with מ and נ in BH and BA. As with all *continuants, there is never a full restriction in the airflow in pronunciation.

nasalization. *n.* (1) The addition of a nasal letter to a word for the sake of pronunciation; (2) the conversion of a letter's pronunciation to that of a nasal pronunciation. The pronunciation of the double *gamma*s in Greek as an *ng* sound in which the airflow proceeds through the nostrils rather than through the mouth would be considered nasalization.

nascent. *adj.* Incomplete, often with the sense of imperfect, as with the *imperfect conjugation.

Nash Papyrus. *n.* A fragment containing the Ten Commandments and part of the *Shema* (Deut 6:4). Found in 1902 and dated to the latter part of the first century A.D., it was the oldest extant Hebrew *manuscript until the discovery of the *Qumran manuscripts.

natural variation. *See* variation.

near demonstrative. *n.* A pronominal that points to an object in close proximity to the speaker; also referred to as an immediate demonstrative. BH has the masculine demonstrative זֶה, "this," the feminine זֹאת, "this," and the common plural אֵלֶּה, "these." Jöüon §§36, 143; MNK §36.2; GKC §§34, 136; *IBHS* §17. *See also* far demonstrative.

Nebiim. *n.* The Hebrew term for "Prophets," referring to the second of the three divisions of the Hebrew canon: the Torah (Law), Nebiim (Prophets) and the Ketubim (Writings). Their initial letters form the *acronym *Tanak.

necessary constituent. *See* obligatory constituent.

negative. *n.* (1) Any free or bound morpheme that connotes the negation of a predicate; (2) any sentence or clause that makes a negative statement.

negative clause. *n.* A clause that conveys some type of negation, either of a *finite or *volitive circumstance. In BH, both nominal and verbal clauses may be negated. The most common particles for negation are לֹא and אַל, though there are others (e.g., Num 23:19: לֹא אִישׁ אֵל וִיכַזֵּב, "God is not a man that he should lie"). BH is unique in that the *imperative *mood may not be used to form a negative command, which requires a volitive plus a *negative *particle. Jöüon §§ 152, 160.

negator. *See* negative.

Neo-Assyrian. *n.* A form of Akkadian that flourished in northern Mesopotamia between 1000-600 B.C. and was written in syllabic cuneiform.

Neo-Babylonian. *n.* A form of Akkadian that flourished in southern

Mesopotamia from about 1000 B.C. to the beginning of the Christian era.

Neo-Punic. *See* Punic.

nesigah. נְסִיגָה, "retreat." —*n.* A BH accentual rule in which a receding of *stress takes place for the purposes of pronunciation and rhythm. In such cases, the stress on the penultima (**milra*) is shifted to the ultima (**milel*), often because of being followed by a *monosyllabic word joined by a *maqqeph (called **athe merachiq*).

neutral imperfect. *n.* Certain instances in which the BH *imperfect and *jussive are inflectionally indistinguishable.

neutrum. *n.* A pronoun that is characteristically vague, ambiguous or generic in reference; also referred to as a vague referent. Its function is more grammatically conventional than necessary, and the nomenclature denotes a sort of neutral sense of reference. In BH, this is most often accomplished by the use of some feminine pronoun, such as in Joshua 10:13: הֲלֹא־הִיא כְתוּבָה עַל־סֵפֶר הַיָּשָׁר, "Is *it* not written in the Book of Yashar?" *See also* pleonastic.

New Criticism. *n.* A literary criticism that focuses primarily on the text, with less regard to historical context, authorial intention and the like. *See also* structuralism, linguistic.

New Hebrew. *n.* Outdated term for Mishnaic Hebrew; not to be confused with Modern Hebrew. *See also* Mishnaic Hebrew.

nikud. *See* vowel pointing.

Niphal stem. *n.* The simple passive verbal stem in BH, which is marked by the נ *preformative. It generally denotes either *passive or *reflexive action. Less common uses of the Niphal include the *tolerative, the *reciprocal and even a *middle use. Joüon §51; MNK §16.3; GKC §51.

nomen, nomina. *See* noun.

nomen rectum. *See* governing element.

nomen regens. *See* governing element.

nomen unitatis. *See* singulative.

nominal. *n.* A noun or other part of speech that behaves as a *substantive (e.g., "The *car* is old"; "*The raising of sheep* is fun"). *See also* verbal.

nominal apposition. *See* apposition.

nominal clause. *n.* A clause formed by identifying or modifying one nominal with another nominal or adjective. Often referred to as a *verbless clause, predicate nominative or subject complement. In English a nominal clause is formed through the use of a linking verb (*copula) such as *is, are, am, were* or *was,* but in BH usually by simple *juxtaposition (e.g., Ex 3:6: אָנֹכִי אֱלֹהֵי אָבִיךָ, "I am the God of your father"). BH sometimes forms nominal clauses by the use of the third-person pronoun, known as the *pronominal copula. There are two types of nominal clauses: the identifying clause and the classifying clause. Both also sometimes use the copulative pronoun. In BH, the identifying clause has a subject plus predicate word order, while the classifying clause has a predicate plus subject word order. Joüon §154; MNK §§12.4, 34.2-3; GKC §§140-141; *IBHS* §8.4.

nominal coordination. *n.* The syntactical linking of nouns together by conjunctives or *juxtaposition. *See also* waw-conjunctive; inclusive coordination.

nominal predicate. *See* nominal clause.

nominal preformative. *n.* Any consonant added to a Semitic *root word in a nominal *pattern to form a Semitic noun. BH uses five nominal preformatives: א, ה, י, מ and ת. *See also* preformative *mem.*

nominal sentence. *See* nominal clause.

nominalization. *n.* The formation of a noun from any other part of speech, such as a verb or adjective.

nominative absolute. *See casus pendens.*

nominative case. *n.* The grammatical noun case that indicates the subject of a sentence. For example, in "Tom is a pilot," the word *Tom* is the subject and thus nominative. *See also* case.

nominative of direct address. *See* vocative.

nonanimate. *n.* A referent that is neither a concrete object (*inanimate) nor living (*animate) but is a mere abstract idea, concept or emotion (e.g., love, peace, joy, hate, Marxism, democracy); also called an abstract.

nonexistence. *See* particle of nonexistence.

nonfinite verb. *n.* A verb that does not take verbal person and does not express action in real time. Nonfinite verbs may also be classed as verbal nouns and would include participles and infinitives. *See also* finite verb.

nongraded. *See* graded.

nonindicatives. *See* volitive moods.

nonsyllabic vowel. *See* glide.

North Arabic. *n.* The most prominent member of the Southwest Semitic family of languages; also commonly referred to as Classical Arabic. It is attested beginning in about A.D. 600, is the language of the Qur'an, and is the basis for most modern Arabic dialects.

North Semitic. *n.* An outdated classification for the Semitic dialects of northern Syria, such as Aramaic and Syriac, which are now classified under the rubric of Northwest Semitic languages.

Northeast Semitic. *n.* The Semitic dialects spoken in ancient Mesopotamia, such as Old Akkadian, various phases of Babylonian and Assyrian.

Northwest Semitic. *n.* The Semitic languages native to Syria-Palestine. They are subdivided into two major classes: the so-called Canaanite dialects (BH, Phoenician, Moabite) and Aramaic.

nota accusativi. See direct-object marker.

noun. *n.* Any existential person, object, emotion or theoretical idea that a predicate may be applied to in communication. There are essentially four grammatical types of nouns: *proper, *common, *collective and *compound. There are three theoretical types of nouns: *animates, *inanimates and *nonanimates. All nouns are of one of two types: *primitive, which cannot be found to have come from another word; and *derivative, which are derived from another word, such as *denominatives or *deverbatives (from a verb). Joüon §§86-93; MNK §§11.2, 23-24; GKC §§79-82; *IBHS* §§5-7.

noun clause. *See* nominal clause.

noun phrase. *n.* A complete subject that includes all of its modifiers but does not possess any form of predication. For example, in "The red-brick building with white pillars was built in 1806," the noun is modified by the definite article "the," by "brick," which is modified by "red," and by the prepositional phrase "with white pillars." All this makes up the noun phrase "The red-brick building with white pillars."

novella. *n.* A tale or short story that is told simply for its interest's sake. The term was used by Martin Dibelius in his form-critical analysis of Mark but has also been used in Old Testament *literary criticism to describe books such as Jonah and Ruth.

Novelle. *n.* A German term for *novella.

nuanced *shewa.* *n.* A linguistic term used to refer to *compound *shewa.* Joüon §9.

nuclear elements. *See* obligatory constituent.

number. *n.* The indication of a word's singularity or plurality. BH has three classes of number: singular, plural and dual. The dual is reserved mostly for natural body pairs. The number marking of BH includes the following suffixes: masculine singular = zero morpheme (no termination); masculine plural = ; feminine singular = ; feminine plural = ; and dual = . Joüon §§90, 135-136; MNK §24.3; GKC §§87-88; *IBHS* §7.

numeral adjective. *n.* An adjective that indicates a definite group being referred to (e.g., "*many* men," "*none* of them").

numeral. *n.* A figure, letter or word that expresses a *number. There are four classes of numerals in English: cardinals (one, two, etc.), ordinal numeral adjectives, which indicate successive order of arrangement (first, second, etc.); ordinal numeral adverbs, which express an order of differing verbal actions (first, secondly, etc.); and iterative numeral adverbs, which expresses the number of occurrences of an action (once, twice, etc.). BH has only cardinal and ordinal numerals but may carry the other connotations based upon use and context.

nun demonstrativum. *See* paragogic *nun.*

nun energicum. *See* paragogic *nun.*

nun epentheticum. *See* paragogic *nun.*

nun inversum. *See* inverted *nun.*

nun paragogicum. *See* paragogic *nun.*

nunation. *n.* The tendency of some Semitic languages to add a *nun* to a word for the purposes of *morphology or smoothing pronunciation.

O

oath formula. *n.* A stereotypical or fixed utterance used to introduce the speech act of oath taking, often accompanied by divine sanctions for nonperformance. In the Hebrew Bible, this is closely linked with self-imprecation (*asseveration) and is most often expressed by the *cohortative. GKC §149.

object. *n.* A sentence nominal that receives the verbal action either as a *direct object or an *indirect object.

object clause. *n.* A clause that takes the role of the *direct object in a sentence (e.g., Gen 6:5: וַיַּרְא יְהוָה כִּי רַבָּה רָעַת הָאָדָם, "And YHWH saw *that the wickedness of humans was great*"). GKC §157. *See also* subject clause.

object complement. *See* double accusative; complement.

object of the infinitive. *n.* A noun or noun phrase that is the object of the action expressed by an infinitive (e.g., "I want to praise *God*").

object of the preposition. *n.* The noun or pronoun that is governed by a preposition (e.g., "unto *him*"; "into *the house*").

objective. *adj.* Pertaining to an *object (accusative) of a clause.

objective case. *See* accusative.

objective genitive. *n.* A genitival relationship in which the governing noun *(regens)* expresses an action, state or state of mind in reference to the governed noun *(rectum)*, such as אֵימַת יְהוָה, "fear of YHWH." Joüon §129. *See also* construct state.

object(ive) pronoun. *n.* (1) A pronoun that acts as the object of a verb; (2) In BH, a suffixed pronoun or the direct-object pronoun formed by the suffixed pronouns attached to the *direct-object marker (e.g., second masculine singular: אוֹתְךָ).

obligatory constituent. *n.* A sentence constituent needed to fill a necessary syntagmatic slot. For example, a sentence with a transitive verb needs an object to complete the thought, so a direct object is considered obligatory. *See also* *adjunct.

oblique case. *n.* In classical grammar, any case other than the nominative or vocative. Stoic philosophers distinguished between the upright and oblique cases. The upright case included the basic nominative (and vocative), and the oblique any other cases, such as *genitive, *dative and so forth. The term is also used more narrowly for the genitive case.

occidental. *adj.* With regard to rabbinics, pertaining to the ancient Hebrew talmudic scholarship located in Palestine. *See also* oriental.

occlusive. *See* stop.

ode. *n.* A song or poem.

Official Aramaic. *See* Aramaic.

old accusative ending. *n.* Outdated nomenclature for *locative *he* (הָ).

old accusative *he.* Outdated nomenclature for **locative *he* (הָ).

Old Akkadian. *n.* A Semitic language attested in Mesopotamia about 2500-2000 B.C. and written in *syllabic cuneiform.

Old Aramaic. *n.* An earlier dialect of *Aramaic from which the latter dialects such as Imperial Aramaic and BA stemmed. This dialect is commonly dated to approximately the tenth century B.C.

Old Assyrian. *n.* A Semitic dialect of Assyrian that flourished 2000-1500 B.C. as a dialect of Akkadian and was epigraphically represented in *syllabic cuneiform.

Old Babylonian. *n.* A dialect of Akkadian which flourished in southern Mesopotamia about 2000-1500 B.C. and was written in *syllabic cuneiform. It is considered by Semitic scholars to be the classical form of Akkadian.

Old Hebrew Script. *See* Phoenician script.

Old Persian. *See* Persian.

onomasticon. *n.* A formal list of proper names found in some ancient literature.

onomatopoeia. *n.* Gk. "to make a name." —*n.* (1) The naming of something after its sound, such as "smack" or "swish." This is used not only of verbs but also of nouns. For example, זְבוּב *(zevuv)* is the BH word for a fly, and the name is probably derived from an imitation of the insect's sound. (2) Literary onomatopoeia is a subtle technique of composing a strophe to reflect sounds that are reminiscent of the utterance's subject matter.

online. *See wayyiqtol.*

opacity, opaqueness. *n.* The case of a word having no natural relationship to its referent and lacking an obvious reason for its use in reference to an object or concept. This is more common with abstracts such as love or time. Contrast with *transparency.

open syllable. *n.* A syllable that consists of a consonant followed by a vowel (CV); also referred to as a simple syllable. Because the syllable ends with a vowel, it generally takes a long vowel, whether the tone syllable or not. *See also* closed syllable.

opposition. *n.* The setting of ideas, concepts, objects, grammatical elements and even clauses in a contrary relationship.

optative clause. *n.* A clause that conveys a wish or strong desire, often with the force of a command, but always with some doubt to its fulfillment (in distinction from a full imperative). Optative clauses are most often formed in BH by the use of the *cohortative and the *jussive moods, though the *imperfect and the *imperative may also be used. Joüon §163; GKC §151.

optative mood. *n.* A *volitive mood that expresses possibility rather than surety, irreal conditions, or a wish or desire with a measure of doubt as to its fulfillment. The optative is often contrasted with the *subjunctive, which expresses a wish or desire with a high level of probability.

optional constituent. *See* adjunct.

oral. *adj.* A linguistic classification referring to phonemes primarily pronounced through the faculties of the mouth such as the sound *p*; To be contrasted with *nasal phonemes like *n* or *m*.

oratio obliqua. *See* indirect discourse.

oratio recta. *See* direct discourse.

ordinal adverb. *See* ordinal numeral.

ordinal numeral. *n.* A number that describes a noun as being at some point in a succession (e.g., first, second, third). *See also* cardinal numerals; numeral.

oriental. *adj.* (1) Generally a term used in the West to refer to the East; (2) the Babylonian school of talmudic scholarship. *See also* Talmud.

orthography. *n.* The scientific study of spelling.

orthophonic *dagesh.* *n.* The rare occurrence of a *dagesh lene* in a non-*begadkepat* letter in order to mark the beginning of a new syllable or to distinguish two consecutive identical consonants to prevent doubling.

ostracon. *n.* A broken potsherd that was used in Syria-Palestine for writing a quick note or a short, less-formal text. Among the more significant finds in Northwest Semitic *epigraphy are the *Samaria ostraca, the *Arad ostraca, and the *Lachish letters. *pl.* ostraca.

otheh merachoq. *See athe merachiq.*

override. *n.* The (implied) carrying over of a grammatical constituent's influence to other parts of the sentence. For example, BH grammarians speak of a preposition override when one preposition actually modifies two or more words, phrases. or poetic strophes. *See also* ellipsis.

P

P. An abbreviation for the Priestly source. *See also* JEDP

Pael. *n.* The Aramaic *active *factitive stem that can also indicate *intensive or *causative ideas. It is similar to that of BH Piel.

palatal. *n.* A *phoneme that exhibits a hard pronunciation with the mouth's palate, such as פ (hard *q*), ג *(g)* and כ *(k)*; sometimes used more loosely as another term for guttural letters. Palatals are distinguished from alveolars in that they are pronounced farther back in the mouth.

palato-alveolar. *adj.* Pertaining to a phoneme articulated in the region between the palate and alveoli.

paleography. *n.* The study of ancient writing for various purposes, such as deciphering and reading scripts, the study of a language or dating of a text or lithograph. The term also subsumes *epigraphy, though they are sometimes used synonymously.

Palestinian Talmud. *See* Talmud.

Palestinian Targum. *n.* One of the most used *targumic traditions, originating in the scribal schools of Palestine. A complete copy named *Neofiti I* was found in 1957, and it includes 450 parchment folios.

palimpsest. *n.* A manuscript that has been used more than once, essentially one that has had a previous text rubbed off its surface and a new one written over it.

papyrus. *n.* A writing material used in ancient Egypt made from the split and dried stalks of the papyrus plant. It was used from the third millennium B.C. well into the common era.

parablepsis. *n.* A scribal error caused by similarities in the beginnings of words. A scribe's eye would often jump from one cluster of letters or words to another similar cluster farther ahead, leaving an omission in the new copy.

paradigmatic relations. *n.* (1) In *phonology, all the sounds that may occur with a particular sound in a given phonetic context; (2) in semantics, a word's relationship to other words closely associated with it. For example, the term *car* shares the same paradigm of thought as *steering wheel, tires, road, automobile* and the like. One is then likely to find such words in the same linguistic context. *See also* syntagmatics.

paradox. *n.* A literary technique that expresses a truth in terms seemingly contradictory on the surface but upon further investigation and meditation may reveal more than expected.

paraenesis. *n.* Exhortation or instruction in ethical behavior.

paraenetic. *adj.* Relating to exhortative or homiletical literature, especially of a moralistic flavor. Deuteronomy is known for its paraenetic discourses.

paragoge. *n.* The addition of an extra phoneme at the end of a word.

paragogic *he.* *n.* (1) The addition of the letter ה to end of a word, usually for phonetic purposes. (2) Sometimes this term is used to refer the locative *he*, which indicates direction or location (e.g., to, toward, at). Joüon §93a-k.

paragogic *nun.* *n.* The placing of a נ before or after an object pronoun, apparently for smoothing pronunciation; also called euphonic *nun*. It is believed to be a remnant from an earlier stage in the language, possibly like the *energic mood in Ugaritic, Classical Arabic and at Amarna. However, some grammarians have separated them as distinct phenomena. In BH it is found primarily in earlier texts and *pausal forms, shows no evidence of *semantic value, and is always in the *tone syllable.

paragogic vowels. *n.* A general classification for several vowel *morphemes that are added to the end of the BH nouns for a variety of reasons. Joüon §93.

paralipomenon. Gk. "that which is left out." —*n.* The *Septuagintal term for 1 and 2 Chronicles, which were viewed as left out and used in a supplementary fashion to Samuel-Kings.

parallelism. *n.* A common BH poetic literary device in which the second line corresponds in some way to the first. For a long time the conception of BH parallelism was dominated by the work of Robert Lowth, who categorized it into three main types: *synonymous, *antithetic and *synthetic. However, modern linguistic studies have provided a significantly more nuanced and globalized reflection on parallelism in the HB. *See also* chiastic sentence; climactic parallelism; emblematic parallelism; inclusio.

paranesis. *See* paraenesis.

paranetic. *See* paraenetic.

parashah. *n.* A liturgical division in the Pentateuch from the Babylonian rabbinic tradition. They are marked in the MT margins by פרש, dividing the Pentateuch into fifty-four annual readings for synagogue worship, and are always located in the inside margin of a *codex manuscript. *See also* seder.

parashiyyot. *n.* Masoretic paragraph divisions in the MT that are indicated by a line space.

paratactic. *adj.* Pertaining to *parataxis.

parataxis. *n.* (1) The coordination of sentence elements by simple *juxtaposition without a coordinating particle such as a *conjunction. It is common in BH poetry. (2) The term may also refer to the juxtaposition of sentences and literary units. *See also* coordination.

parchment. *n.* Animal skins that were prepared to be writing materials in ancient times. They were bound into both scroll and codex forms.

parenesis. *See* paraenesis.

parenthesis. *n.* A thought or a grammatically complete sentence within a sentence that is not crucial to meaning. If a parenthesis is removed, the basic sentence retains coherent meaning.

parity treaty. *See* treaty.

parole. *n.* A term coined by Ferdinand de Saussure to refer to a language system as it is applied and used by an individual. It is to be distinguished from *langue,* which is a system of language itself that exerts influence on an individual.

paronomasia. *n.* A play on words developed from a proper name. For example, Malachi 3:6-9 contains a wordplay on the name יַעֲקֹב, "Jacob," and עקב, "defraud, swindle." *See also* repetition.

paronym. *n.* A word that shares a root with another word (e.g., כתב, "to write," and מכתב, "writing").

parse. *v.* To assign words to their proper part of speech, usually analyzing them so as to remove all *bound morphemes until only the seminal *free morpheme remains.

participial noun. *See* gerund.

participial phrase. *n.* A phrase that is introduced by a participle, such as, "*Walking* into the room, she saw her father."

participium tantum. *n.* A verb that has a participial form in a language but is otherwise not attested as having a *finite form.

participle. *n.* A verbal noun that can function either as a verb or as an adjective. The term was coined by the second-century grammarian Dionysius Thrax to define words that participate in the attributes of nouns and verbs. English has present participles expressed by the -ing ending and often aided by a copula (verb of being; e.g., "He is *sleeping*") and past participles expressing completed action with an -ed ending and helping verbs (*have, has*, etc.; e.g., "I have *walked* a long distance"). BH has two forms of the participle in the Qal stem: active and passive. They may perform both nominally and verbally. Joüon §§50, 121; MNK §§15.8, 20.3; GKC §§50, 116; *IBHS* §37.

particle. *n.* An indeclinable word that is added to a syntactical construction to modify or clarify the meaning in some way; also known as a *form word. BH particles include *locative *he* (הָ), the particle of entreaty נָא, the particles of existence יֵשׁ and nonexistence אֵין, prepositions, conjunctions, and interjections such as הִנֵּה. Joüon §§102-105; MNK §§38-45; GKC §§99-105.

particle of entreaty. *n.* A particle found with volitives and imperatives and expressing the idea of "please" or a sense of urgency in what is being communicated (נָא).

particle of existence. *n.* A BH particle that means "there is" (יֵשׁ). The particle of existence was originally a noun and thus can be used with both genders and numbers. Its function is much like that of the Eng. *copulative. BA also has an analogous particle of existence: אִיתַי. *See also* particle of nonexistence; existential clause.

particle of nonexistence. *n.* A BH particle that means "there is not" (אַיִן; construct אֵין). Like the BH *particle of existence, it may be used with both genders and numbers. BA does not have a separate particle of nonexistence but rather negates the particle of existence (e.g., לָא אִיתַי, "there is not, there does not exist"). *See also* existential clause.

partitive. *n.* An expression or grammatical construction that identifies an item as a part of a whole. In both BH and BA, this is often accomplished by use of the מִן preposition (e.g., 2 Kings 9:33: "And *some* of her blood was sprinkled on the wall"; Dan 6:2 [MT 3]: [lit. "one *from* them"]).

partitive genitive. *n.* An objective genitive relationship such as the construct state in BH to indicate a partitive idea (e.g., 2 Chron 21:17: קְטֹן בָּנָיו, "youngest of his sons"). Joüon §29f. *See also* partitive; construct state; objective genitive; subjective genitive.

parts of speech. *n.* The basic classes of words as grouped according to grammatical function. There are generally eight classified parts of speech: nouns, pronouns, adjectives, verbs, adverbs, prepositions, conjunctions and interjections. Semitic languages add the class of *particles for all elements that cannot be properly classified in any of these eight.

passive voice. *n.* The *voice of a verb in which the action is committed upon the subject and does not have a direct object. The nominal entity that commits the action of a passive verb is called an *agent.

past perfect. *See* pluperfect.

pastiche. *n.* The composing of a communication or literary work by employing familiar phrases or expressions from other literary works. This phenomenon is common in religious circles that share a canon, such as how phrases from the Bible are used in sermons and theological writings. *See also* adornment.

patach. *n.* A vowel sign of the *masoretic pointing system (ַ) that has an *a*-class vowel sound. *See also* furtive *patach*.

patach furtivum. *See* furtive *patach*.

patach furtive. *See* furtive *patach*.

patient. *n.* Any nominal element that is the recipient of the verbal action. This may be both the *object of an *active verb or the *subject of a *passive verb. The linguistic classification of a patient is further subdivided into the *affected element or the *effected element.

patronym. *n.* A personal name derived from an ancestor, often by the addition of a prefix or suffix. *See also* toponym.

pattern. *n.* The phenomena of Semitic languages to use vowel patterns with the consonantal roots to give various shades of meaning.

patterning. *n.* The use of parallel patterns in the Hebrew Bible for poetic and aesthetic appeal. Patterning functions on the lexical, phonological and strophic levels. Common patterns include aabb, abab and abba (chiastic).

pausal form. *n.* The form of a BH word in the MT as it appears in its pausal state, with all pertinent vowel changes and accent. *See also* pause.

pausal lengthening. *See* pause.

pause. *n.* The final word of a verse or clause in the MT which is marked by a major accentual stop and receives *tone-syllable vowel lengthening. The two major accents used to mark a pausal form are: *silluq,* a short vertical line appearing under the word; and *atnach,* an upside-down v-shape (֑) under the word that marks the halfway point of a verse.

peak. *n.* The climax or goal of a narrative. *See also* prepeak; postpeak.

Peal. The Aramaic ground verbal stem conveying the active voice.

pe-aleph. *n.* A weak verb with an א in the word-initial position of the triliteral root; also called a I-*aleph* verb. Joüon §73; MNK §18.3; GKC §68.

***pe*-guttural.** *n.* A weak verb with a guttural letter in the word-initial position of the triliteral root; also called I-guttural verbs (e.g., עזר). Joüon §§67-68; MNK §18.2; GKC §§63, 68.

Peil. *n.* The Aramaic vowel-stem conjugation that expresses the *passive voice of the regular ground stem (*Peal).

***pe*-laryngeal.** *See pe*-guttural.

***pendens* construction.** *See casus pendens.*

pendent. *adj.* Relating to any element attached to a sentence (usually sentence-initial) that has no formal grammatical relation to it. *See also casus pendens.*

pendent nominative. *See casus pendens.*

Pentateuch. *n.* The first five books of the Hebrew Bible: Genesis, Exodus, Leviticus, Numbers and Deuteronomy. It is referred to in Judaism as the Torah and is the first of the three divisions of the Hebrew canon. *See also* Tanak.

pe-nun. *n.* A weak verb with a נ in the word-initial position of the triliteral root; also called a I-*nun* verb (e.g., נפל). Joüon §72; MNK §18.6; GKC §66.

***pe-nun* and *lamed*-guttural.** *n.* A weak verb with a נ in the word-initial position and a guttural letter in the final position of the triliteral root (e.g., נגא).

perfect. *n.* A finite verbal form denoting completed action; contrast with *imperfect.

perfective conjugation. *n.* The suffix conjugation in BH and in the Semitic languages, which is characterized by the addition of pronominal sufformatives. It focuses on the completeness of action rather than on time of action and therefore lends itself to a multiplicity of possible translations, though usually with a past-tense nuance, that must be discerned from syntax and context. Joüon

§§42, 112; MNK §§15.1, 19.1-2; GKC §§44, 106; *IBHS* §30. *See also* imperfect.

perfect of certainty. *See* prophetic perfect.

perfective of confidence. *See* prophetic perfect.

perfective of prayer. *See* precative perfect(ive).

performative. *See* performative utterance.

performative utterance. *n.* A statement that is an action in and of itself, such as "I forgive you" or Genesis 6:18: "But I establish my covenant with you."

pericope. Gk. "cut around." —*n.* A short passage, unit or discourse from a literary composition. The term can be applied to a paragraph or even a literary scene.

peripeteia. *n.* A sudden and unexpected change of events or circumstances in a literary work; it is closely associated with irony (e.g., the sudden downfall and demise of the *antagonist Haman in the book of Esther).

peripheral element. *See* adjunct.

periphrasis. *n.* The use of many words rather than just a few in communication; the use of a phrase or group of words rather than grammar to convey an idea (e.g., "did walk" compared with just "walked"). *See also* circumlocution.

periphrastic chain. *n.* A group of words or a phrase used to convey a single idea that may often be conveyed more simply.

periphrastic verb. *See* auxiliary verb.

permansive. *n.* A state of being or condition of reality. This term is used like *factitive,* especially in reference to D stems.

permutation. *n.* A subclass of nominal apposition in which the second noun further defines rather than merely complements a preceding noun (e.g., Gen 9:4: אַךְ־בָּשָׂר בְּנַפְשׁוֹ דָמוֹ לֹא תֹאכֵלוּ, "But the flesh with its life, *its blood,* you shall not eat").

Persian. *n.* The language of the ancient Achaemenid Empire before its demise at the hand of Alexander of Macedon in 332 B.C.; often referred to as Old Persian. It is the predecessor of Modern Persian (Iranian), which grew out of the Middle Persian of the seventh to eighth centuries A.D.

person. *n.* The distinction between grammatical roles in discourse that mark a speaker (first person, "I, we"), an addressee (second person, "you") and other persons, objects or ideas described (third person, "he, she, it, they").

personal pronoun. *n.* A *cataphoric element used in place of a noun to avoid repetition that indicates person (first, second or third person), such as he, she, it, you or they. Personal pronouns point to an *antecedent noun. BH has an array of personal pronouns divided into *independent personal pronouns (may stand alone) and *dependent personal pronouns (*sufformatives). These are further subdivided into *object pronouns (directly suffixed to verbs according to special rules) and *possessives (suffixed to nouns and indicate a *genitive relationship). Joüon §§39, 146; MNK §36.1; GKC §§32, 135; *IBHS* §16.

personification. *n.* The attribution of human characteristics to an animal, *inanimate or *nonanimate.

pesher. *n.* (1) An *intertestamental and New Testament–period rabbinic interpretational method that emphasized present fulfillment of prophetic or other literature, with the implied supernatural illumination of the interpreter; (2) a document characterized by this type of interpretation. *pl.* pesherim.

Peshitta. *n.* A *Syriac translation of the Christian Bible dating from the fourth to fifth centuries A.D. and used among the Syrian Orthodox churches. The Peshitta lacks 2 Peter, 2 and 3 John, Jude and Revelation, all of which the Syrian church rejected.

petuchah. *n.* The insertion of a letter פ into the text of the MT to mark an "open" paragraph ending, which was traditionally followed by a full line-space. It is used in conjunction with a ס, called a *setumah,* to indicate a "closed" paragraph ending. However, their use had become inconsistent by the time of the Leningrad Codex, and so their use in BHS is also inconsistent.

Pe-waw, pe-yod. *n.* A weak verb with a ו or י in the word-initial position of the triliteral root; also called a I-*waw* or a I-*yod* verb (e.g., ישׁב). Joüon §§74-77; MNK §18.7; GKC §§69-71.

pharyngeal. *n.* A letter pronounced by a restriction of the airway by the pharynx, possessing glottal characteristics. Pharyngeals in BH are represented by the *unvoiced *glottal *fricative ח and the *voiced *velar fricative ע. Joüon §5j-l.

pharyngeal fricative. *See* pharyngeal.

phatic. *adj.* Descriptive of communication comprising a speech-act that intrinsically establishes or preserves a relationship of some sort between the conversants, such as an oath or covenant.

Phenician. *See* Phoenician.

philology. *See* comparative philology.

Phoenician. *n.* A dialect of the Northwest Semitic family of language having close affinity to BH, Moabite, the Canaanitisms of the Amarna archives and Ugaritic. It was the spoken language of the seafaring Phoenicians, whose major cites were Tyre, Sidon, Byblos and later Carthage.

phoneme. *n.* The smallest theoretical sound unit of a language that articulates meaning. Phonemes are distinguished by comparing two words that sound similar except for one sound. If that one sound makes a change in meaning, then that sound is a phoneme. For example, *can* and *cat* sound similar, yet the differing third letter changes the meaning to another word. It is worth noting that a phoneme is not the actual usage of a sound, but is a theoretical abstraction. The actual usage, which can be recorded and analyzed by machines, is called a phone.

phonemics. *n.* The study of a language as a complete system of sounds available to the speaker for effective communication. The peculiar ways in which a given language puts together its distinctive minimal speech sounds and accents is called a phonemic system.

phonetics. *n.* The study of speech sounds as they are actually pronounced. It is further subdivided into two fields: acoustic phonetics (the study of sound waves) and articulatory phonetics (the study of how certain sounds are produced by speech organs).

phonogram. *n.* A writing sign employed to represent a sound, such as the letters *a, b* and *c*.

phonology. *n.* The discipline of defining all the sounds of a language and its sound patterns. Through this process, the language is broken down into sound units termed *phonemes.

phrasal verb. *n.* An English verbal idea that is a compound of a regular verb and an adverb (e.g., "go down," "come in," or "stand up"). Phrasal verbs are necessary for the translation of some Semitic verbs because of their inherent sense of direction. For example, the BH verb בוֹא requires a translation of "go in" or "come in."

phrase. *n.* A distinct group of words in a sentence construction that act as a unit but have neither a subject nor a predicate. A phrase may act as a *substantive or *modifier, and a phrase includes a *governing word and all its modifiers. Basic types of phrases include *noun phrases, *verb phrases, *prepositional phrases, *participial phrases, *construct phrases (BH) and so forth.

phylum. *n.* Used generally, any grouping in any class or category; in linguistics, a group of dialects that are connected or disconnected. *pl.* phyla.

pictogram. *n.* A picture or picturelike symbol that represents concepts. Pictographic writing dates back to the earliest periods in written language and later evolved into logographic writing.

pictograph. *See* pictogram.

Piel stem. *n.* The active *factitive stem in BH. Its true force has always remained somewhat elusive to Semitic grammarians. The factitive or *declarative quality of the stem is understood as making a declaration or pointing to a state or quality of something. It is characterized by the *doubling of the *medial radical by means of a *dagesh forte, unless the medial radical is a *guttural, in which case the preceding vowel is lengthened. Joüon §52; MNK §16.4; GKC §52.

Pilpel. *n.* The BH inflection of *geminate verbs in the Piel stem in which the entire *diconsonantal root is doubled rather than just the last letter (e.g., גל becomes in גִּלְגַּלְתִּי in the first common singular).

Pirqe Aboth. Mishnaic Hebrew. "Chapters of the Fathers." —*n.* A collection of moral sayings in the *Mishnah that are considered among the oldest material within it.

pisqot. See parashiyyot.

plena. See full writing.

plene writing. *See* full writing.

pleonasm. *n.* (1) A grammatical element that is redundant or unnecessary; a statement or use of an adjective that is tautological; (2) a *dummy element, often used to make sense of a sentence where a subject is indefinite, undefined or unknown. For example, someone trying to convey hearsay may employ a *pleonastic pronoun to make sense of the sentence even though there is no antecedent to it (e.g., "I heard that *they* have found Philip of Macedon's tomb"). In most cases, the same idea could be better expressed by rearrangement of the sentence without the pleonastic pronoun (e.g., "I heard that Philip of Macedon's tomb has been found").

plosion. *n.* A phonetic occurrence where there is a momentary restriction of the air flow followed by a sudden burst of air. *See also* plosive.

plosive. *adj.* or *n.* A linguistic term for consonants that must be pronounced by a temporary compression of air and then a sudden release, resulting in a minor burst of air. BH linguists refer to the **dagesh* of simple plosion *(*dagesh lene)* and the *dagesh* of prolonged plosion *(*dagesh forte)*. Simple plosion is the pronunciation of a single plosive letter, while prolonged plosion is the pronunciation of a doubled letter (e.g., יִפֹּל, "yip-pol"). Joüon §10.

plosive *dagesh.* *See* dagesh lene. *See also* plosive.

plot conflict. *n.* The narrative problem around which the plot is constructed. All narratives are based upon some kind of problem that works toward resolution in the coarse of narration.

plot motif. *n.* A common shaping of a narrative, such as epic, quest, character conflict and the like.

pluperfect. *n.* The expression of a completed action (perfect) in past time. In English it is marked by the **helping verb *had* and should be contrasted with the regular perfect, which expresses completed events in either the not-so-distant past or in contexts in which it does not matter (e.g., perfect: "he ran"; pluperfect: "he had run"). Because of the aspectual nature of BH, the tense of actions must be deduced from a combination of verbal inflection and context in translation.

plural. *adj.* or *n.* Indicating more than one of someone or something. BH nouns have three forms of number: *singular, dual and plural. Because there are both masculine and feminine nouns, there are masculine and feminine forms of plurality marking. The masculine plural morpheme (suffix) is ִים , and the feminine plural morpheme (suffix) is וֹת. Plurality may also be implied by the use of a *collective noun, which is singular in form but always refers to a corporate body of individuals or items. The *dual is also a form of plural but is generally limited to natural body pairs and other unique *lexemes. Joüon §§90, 135-136; MNK §24.3; GKC §§87-88, 124; *IBHS* §7.

plural of majesty. *n.* The BH use of a plural *sufformative in the formation of an *honorific. Though grammatically plural, the word will be found with a singular verb. For example, in Genesis 1:1 the subject *God* is plural, but the verb is masculine singular in form: בְּרֵאשִׁית בָּרָא אֱלֹהִים אֵת הַשָּׁמַיִם וְאֵת הָאָרֶץ, "In the beginning God created the heavens and the earth."

plurale tantum. n. Nouns that are used only in the plural or dual and have no singular form attested. In most cases they are *abstracts (e.g., סַנְוֵרִים, "blindness") or *singulatives (e.g., שָׁמַיִם, "heavens"). Joüon §90f.

pluralis excellentiae. See plural of majesty.

pluralis majestatis. See plural of majesty.

plusquamperfectum. See pluperfect.

poet's dictionary. *n.* A hypothetical deposit of *fixed pairs employed by the "professional poet." Most scholars of BH and Ugaritic poetry now recognize that most fixed pairs occur in prose as well and so the concept of a "poet's dictionary" is for the most part fictitious.

pointing. *See* vowel pointing.

Polal. *n.* The passive intensive (Pual) of *hollow verbs.

polar opposition. *See* opposition.

polarity. *n.* The opposing of two objects or concepts that represent two extremes, such as *heavens* and *earth*.

Polel. The grammatical classification of the *active *factitive conjugation of *hollow verbs in both BH and BA. This is analogous to the Piel in regular strong verbs. It is formed primarily by the *reduplication of the second consonant of a *hollow verb's *biconsonantal root (e.g., the verb קוּם in the Polel is קוֹמֵם).

polyglot. *n.* An edition of the Bible printed with parallel columns of multiple languages (e.g., Origen's Hexapla).

polyphone, polyphony. *n.* Multiple sounds or pronunciations, especially multiple phonemes that possess the same morphological meaning.

polysemy. *n.* In semantics, the existence of more than one meaning.

polysyndeton. *n.* The coordination of an enumerated series by the repetition of conjunctives. In most cases of long enumeration, BH, like English, will place a conjunction only between the last two words. However, there are many cases where each successive item enumerated is joined by a *waw*-conjunction (e.g., Gen 12:16 [6x];

15:19-21 [9x]; 24:35 [7x]; Josh 7:24 [10x]).

polysynthetic language. *n.* A more extreme classification of an agglutinating language. Such languages form expressions by connecting long strings of morphemes into complex words that can express complete sentences. Polysynthetic languages may express even more complex thoughts than characterized by regular agglutinatives. *See also* agglutinative language; isolating language; inflectional language.

positional variant. *See* allophone.

positive degree. *n.* A description of basic *adjectival attribution; also referred to as *absolute degree. However, this term is used specifically to contrast basic adjectival modification with *comparative and *superlative degree. Joüon §141; MNK §30.5; GKC §133; *IBHS* §14.4-5.

possessive adjective. *See* adjective.

possessive case. *See* genitive; construct state.

postconstructus. *n.* The genitive absolute noun following a construct noun. *See* construct state.

postpeak. *n.* The remaining narrative that follows a peak in a narrative sequence. *See also* prepeak; peak.

postpositive, postpositional. *n.* (1) Any masoretic accent that is placed at the end of a word; (2) a grammatical element that *follows* a specified position (i.e., postposition). Suffixes and the BA definite article are examples of postpositive elements. *See also* prepositive.

postverbal field. *n.* The part of a clause that follows the verb. *See also* free inversion.

pragmatics. *n.* The study of utterances between speakers, with emphasis on their contextualization. *See also* utterance.

precative moods. *See* volitive moods.

precative perfect(ive). *n.* The rare use of the BH *suffix conjugation, instead of a volitive, for the expression of entreaty, wish or desire. *See also* volitive moods.

predicate. *n.* The syntagm of the sentence that makes an assertion about the subject. In a *verbal clause, the predicate consists of the verb and all its modifiers. In a *verbless clause (common in BH), the predicate constitutes a state of being rather than a spatiotemporal action.

predicate accusative. *See* direct object.

predicate adjective. *n.* The use of an adjective in the formation of an *existential clause; also referred to as a subject complement or a predicate nominative. In BH, the predicate adjective usually stands before the noun to which it refers and will never take an *article. Thus, it will always agree with the noun in *gender and *number but not necessarily in definiteness. It will agree in definiteness only when the noun is indefinite. *See also* adjective, attributive adjective.

predicate nominative. *n.* In English grammar, a *nominative *substantive that is joined with a linking verb (copula) to form a predicate. In BH, such predication is performed by the pronominal copula, particles of existence or nonexistence, juxtaposition, and sometimes the verb הָיָה, but most often it is accomplished by simple juxtaposition. *See also* predicate adjective.

predicate noun. *See* predicate nominative.

predicative. *adj.* Anything in a grammatical construction that expresses predication.

predicator. *See* verb.

predicators of existence. *See* particle of existence; particle of nonexistence.

prefix. *n.* A bound morpheme attached to the beginning of a word to modify the meaning in some way.

prefix conjugation. *See* imperfect.

prefixed aleph. *See* prosthetic *aleph*.

prefixed preposition. *n.* A preposition that is attached to the beginning of a word. In BH and BA prefixed prepositions include בְּ, לְ, כְּ and sometimes מִן (e.g., מִשָּׁם)

preformative. *See* prefix.

preformative consonant. *n.* The prefixed consonantal gender, number and person markers of the *prefix conjugations (imperfective) of the Semitic languages. *See also* preformative vowel.

preformative mem. *n.* The common prefixed use of the letter *mem* in the formation of various types of Semitic nouns. It is used for implying an instrument of an action (e.g., צוּד, "to hunt, capture," and מָצוֹד, "net") or abstraction (e.g, אָפֵל, "dark," and מַאֲפֵל, "darkness") as well as with verbal roots and stems to form participles (e.g., קְטַל, "to kill," and מְקַטֵּל, "one who kills, murderer").

preformative nominal. *See* nominal preformative.

preformative vowel. *n.* A vowel accompanying the *preformative consonants of the *prefix conjugation (imperfective). For example, with certain I-*aleph* verbs, the preformative vowel becomes *holem* (יֹאמַר). *See also* preformative *consonant.

pregenitive. *n.* A construct noun. It *precedes* the *genitive absolute noun.

pregnant construction. *n.* A figure of speech or idiom that has an implied meaning. The construction is said to be pregnant with expressed meaning. For example, in וּמִקַּרְנֵי רֵמִים עֲנִיתָנִי, "and from the horns of wild beasts *you answered me*" (Ps 22:22), the words "you answered me" imply "you saved me."

prepause. *n.* (1) a syllable preceding a pausal syllable; (2) a word preceding a pausal word. *See also* pause.

prepeak. *adj.* Relating to story elements that precede or lead up to the peak (resolution or climax) in a narrative sequence. During the prepeak sequence, there is plot conflict upon which tension is built, culminating in a narrative resolution. *See also* peak; postpeak.

preposition. *n.* A particle used to indicate the relationship of a substantive to another word or sentence: (e.g., *to, for, with, from, out, in, on, above*). BH uses an array of prepositions, which may be broken into two major classes: *separable prepositions (*free morphemes) and *inseparable prepositions (*bound morphemes). Joüon §§103, 132; MNK §39; GKC §§101-103; *IBHS* §11.

prepositional object. *See* object of the preposition.

prepositional phrase. *n.* A phrase constructed with a preposition as the *governing element *(regens)*, such as "He went *to the store*."

prepositive, prepositional. *n.* (1) Any grammatical element that occurs before a specified position (e.g., a *preposition is in the "pre-position"). *Prefixes of all types are prepositives, in contrast to *suffixes, which are *postpositives. (2) Any *Masoretic accent placed at the beginning of a word. *See also* postpositive, postpositional.

preterit. *See* preterite.

preterite. *n.* (1) In grammar generally, the past tense; (2) more narrowly in Semitic studies, another term for the *suffix conjugation or for the *wayyiqtol*. While the term generically refers to past tense, BH and Semitic languages do not focus as much on tense as they do verbal *aspect.

pretonic. *n.* The syllable immediately preceding the *accented syllable. The accented syllable in BH is called the *tone syllable, so the syllable preceding is named pretonic. The syllable location preceding the pretonic syllable is known as the*propretonic position.

pretonic reduction. *n.* In BH, a vowel reduction pattern affecting the syllable immediately preceding the *tone syllable after the addition of a sufformative. In nouns, a pretonal *tsere* (sometimes *qamets*) reduces to a *shewa* if the pretonic syllable is closed or has an unchangeably long vowel. In verbs, various pretonal vowels reduce to *shewa* (e.g., יִכְתֹּב plus the suffix וּ = יִכְתְּבוּ). *See also* propretonic reduction.

pretonic vowel. *n.* In BH, a preferred vowel, usually a *qamets* but sometimes a *tsere*, that stands in an open syllable preceding the tone syllable.

preverbal field. *n.* The part of a clause that precedes the verb. *See also* free inversion, main field.

Priestly. *adj.* In the *JEDP documentary theory of pentateuchal composition, the pentateuchal source associated with priestly traditions and redaction.

primitive. *adj.* A noun that was not derived from another word but is pure in its origin; to be contrasted with derivative nouns such as *deverbatives, nouns derived from a verb and so on.

principal accent. *n.* The primary accent in a word that also has a *secondary accent.

principal clause. *n.* A main or independent *clause.

principal tone. *n.* The primary accented syllable of a word, to be distinguished from the countertone or secondary accent. *See also* tone syllable; secondary accent; *meteg.*

privation. *n.* The formation of a construction that connotes deprivation of some sort.

privative. *n.* (1) A verb or adverbial element that expresses the removal of something (i.e., privation). The term also refers to prepositional phrases in which the preposition indicates the concept of privation. This is often expressed by the מִן preposition and is a common use of the Piel stem (e.g., Job 21:9: בָּתֵּיהֶם שָׁלוֹם מִפָּחַד, "Their homes are secure *from fear*"). (2) Any word lacking an element.

process morpheme. *n.* A morphological modification (change in meaning) by the process of changing a letter to a different one. *See also* zero morpheme.

proclitic. *adj. See* proclisis.

proclisis. *n.* A word bound to the following word and having no accent of its own. A proclitic word is pronounced with and relies on the accent of the word that follows. In BH this condition is caused by the construct state or by words being joined by a **maqqeph*. Proclisis is also common among BH prepositions and is properly considered to be a *linking condition. Joüon §§13a, 15a.

proclitic *mem.* *n.* In BH, a letter *mem* that is attached to the beginning of a word to become part of the word, usually indicating it to be a noun.

pro-form. *n.* Anything that stands in the place of a noun to reduce redundancy. *See also* anaphora; cataphora.

progressive action. *See* linear action.

progressive assimilation. *n.* The influence of a preceding letter upon the following letter so as to make it like the preceding letter. *See also* regressive assimilation.

progressive parallelism. *See* synthetic parallelism.

prohibition. *n.* A command not to do something. In BH prohibitions are always expressed with a negative particle plus a *volitive form, namely, the *jussive or *cohortative. The *imperative mood cannot be negated in BH.

prohibitive. *adj.* Relating to any morphological or syntactical construction that creates prohibition.

projected parallelism. *See* synthetic parallelism.

prolegomenon. *n.* An introductory treatise or preliminary remarks about a field of study. *pl.* prolegomena.

prolepsis. *n.* (1) A grammatical element that is anticipatory in function. A proleptic element looks forward to something else (*cataphoric). (2) In literary studies, the term is used to denote the *prophetic perfect, as in Amos 5:1-3, where the prophet wails over the fall of Israel as if completed, though it stands in the future.

prolongation. *See* doubling.

prolonged plosion (*dagesh of*). *See* plosion.

prologue. *n.* The beginning section of a literary composition that tends to set the stage or define the context upon which the work is to unfold.

pronomen, pronominia. *See* pronoun.

pronominal. *See* pronoun.

pronominal copula. *See* copula.

pronominal suffixes. *n.* The personal pronoun suffixes that are attached to the end of construct nouns (making the suffixes absolute), to other particles (such as *prepositions), to verbs, and to the *direct object marker אֵת. They are also referred to as *enclitic personal pronouns because they draw the accent away from the construct noun. They convey possession when attached to nouns and play the role of an object when attached to verbs, prepositions and the *direct object marker.

pronominalization. *n.* The change of any nominal or nominal phrase to a *pro-form in order to minimize redundancy (e.g., changing "Anne cut Anne" to "Anne cut herself").

pronoun. *n.* A word to refer back to a noun to avoid redundancy. GKC §§32-37. *See also* anaphora; cataphora; antecedent.

proper noun. A noun considered definite by nature, such as the names of persons and places (e.g., יְרוּשָׁלַיִם, "Jerusalem").

prophetic perfect. *n.* A way of speaking of future events in the *perfect *aspect so as to demonstrate the certainty of their fruition; also referred to as the perfect of certainty, perfective of confidence and accidental perfective. This may be conveyed by both the *perfective conjugation and the *wayyiqtol conjugation.

propretonic. *n.* The syllable two places removed from the tone syllable. Grammarians refer to the *tone syllable (ultima), the *pretonic syllable (penultima) and the propretonic syllable (antipenultima).

propretonic reduction. *n.* In BH, the reduction of a *qamets or *tsere to a *vocal *shewa* in an open propretonic syllable (antipenultima) after the addition of a suffix (e.g., לֵבָב becomes לְבָבוֹת). Such reduction takes place mostly in the conjugation of nouns but sometimes in the inflection of verbs. *See also* pretonic reduction.

prosaic. *adj.* Having the attributes of prose writing style, in contrast to elevated or poetic style. The term may be used with a negative connotation to imply verbosity or wordiness. *See also* prose.

prose. *n.* The most common form of spoken or written communication; straight monologue or dialogue; any type of writing that is not poetic.

prospective element. *See* cataphoric.

prostaxis. *See* parataxis.

prosthesis. *n.* The addition of a *phoneme (usually a vowel) in BH and the Semitic languages to a *word-initial consonant cluster in order to smooth pronunciation, which by itself tends to run contrary to the regular rules of Semitic pronunciation (e.g., BH *zroa*, "arm," becomes *ezroa* or *zeroa*). Prosthetic vowels compensate for a consonant cluster at the beginning of a word, and *anaptyctic vowels compensate for consonant clusters at the end of a word. *See also* prosthetic *aleph.*

prosthetic *aleph.* *n.* A *bound morpheme *aleph* that is found in BH and the Semitic languages added to the beginning of a word for the purpose of smoothing pronunciation, strengthening or transliteration of a foreign word as in Mishnaic Hebrew; also referred to as prothetic *aleph* or a prefixed *aleph* (e.g., אֶזְרוֹעַ, "arm"). Joüon §17a; GKC §19m.

prosthetic *ayin.* *n.* An *ayin* used in the same manner as the *prosthetic *aleph* (e.g., the *ayin* in עַקְרָב, "scorpion"). *See also* prosthesis; prosthetic *aleph.*

prosthetic vowel. *See* prosthesis.

protagonist. *n.* The main character of any narration. *See also* antagonist.

protasis. *n.* The subordinate conditional clause of a conditional sentence. In BH, the protasis is often marked by the conditional particle אִם. *See also* conditional sentence.

prothetic. *See* prosthesis.

protomasoretic text. *n.* A Hebrew Bible text-criticism term referring to manuscripts that stand prior to but in the developmental lineage of the masoretic textual tradition. Primary examples are the extant texts discovered among the Khirbet Qumran library.

Proto-Semitic. *n.* A hypothetical language that has been deduced from the common elements of the multiple Semitic languages.

Proto-Sinaitic. *n.* The language attested in a group of alphabetic inscriptions located in Sinai that were classified by William F. Albright as an early attestation of the Northwest Semitic branch of the Semitic languages and dated to about 1500 B.C. Recently alphabetic writing has been attested as early as 1900 B.C. at Wadi el-Hol in Egypt.

protolanguage. *n.* Any unattested language from which a family of languages necessarily was derived (e.g., *Proto-Semitic).

provenance. *n.* The location in which something originated. In biblical studies, the term is used primarily of literary works.

proverbial perfective. *See* gnomic perfective.

proxemics. *n.* A linguistic subdiscipline that studies communication in reference to the physical proximity of the conversants.

Psalter. *n.* The canonical book of Psalms in the Hebrew Bible.

Pseudepigrapha. Gk. "false writings." —*n.* A large collection of Hellenistic Jewish writings that were considered important but not *canonical.

pseudepigraphic. *adj.* Relating to any writing or to any of a special collection of ancient Jewish writings that were written under a false name, usually named after an important figure in religious tradition for the sake of lending authority to the work.

pseudogeminate verbs. *n.* A classification of BA verbs that exhibit characteristics of regular *geminates but cannot truly be classified as geminate. Examples of such may be seen in the BA words הלך and סלק, which undergo the elision of the medial-position ל in some *binyanim.

pseudo-Hiphil. *n.* A secondary class of the Hiphil verb stem that, although having the inflectional accidence of the causative stem, actually conveys the force of a *Qal. Joüon §55f.

pseudonym. *n.* A false name.

pseudonymous. *adj.* Written under a false name.

psychological factitive. *See* delocutive.

Pual stem. *n.* The factitive passive stem of the BH *binyanim. It is built on the analogy of the *Piel stem but expresses passivity. Joüon §56; MNK §16.5; GKC §52.

puncta extraordinaria. *See* extraordinary points.

punctiliar action. *n.* Verbal action viewed as a point or as occurring once in time and then ceasing; to be contrasted with *linear action and *frequentive action.

punctual. *See* punctiliar action.

Punic. *n.* A later dialect of Phoenician associated with the settlement at Carthage. Classical Punic was used from about the fifth century

B.C. to 146 B.C. (the Roman destruction of Carthage). A dialect known as Neo-Punic continued in use until the sixth century A.D.

pure stem. *See* Qal stem.

purpose clause. *n.* A *subordinate clause that expresses an action giving purpose to the action of the *main clause. In English a purpose clause would use coordinating conjunctives such as *that, in order that, so that, for, for the sake of, to* or *in order to.* They are also referred to as *telic or final purpose clauses. They can be expressed in BH by the use of the particles לְ, לְמַעַן, בַּעֲבוּר, אֲשֶׁר, לְבִלְתִּי (for negatives) or the *waw*-conjunctive (e.g., הֶעֱמַדְתִּיךָ בַּעֲבוּר הַרְאֹתְךָ אֶת־כֹּחִי, "I let you stand *in order to demonstrate my power*"). Joüon §168; GKC §165.

Q

Qal passive. *n.* The use of the Qal with a minor vowel variation to indicate passivity (*internal passive). It has traditionally been confused in the perfect with the *Pual (קֻטַּל) and in the imperfect with the *Hophal (הָקְטַל). It is difficult to distinguish between these in the text itself. In order to see if a certain word is Qal passive or not, one should look to see what the root's normal active stem is. In other words, if a word in the passive-perfect has the Piel for its active form, then it is a Pual; if a passive-imperfect word has the Hiphil for its active, then it is a Hophal. However, if one of these two forms has a Qal for its active form, it is a Qal passive. Joüon §58; MNK §16.2; GKC §§52e, 53u.

Qal stem. קַל, "light." —*n.* In BH, the the simple active *verbal form; also called the B-stem, base stem, G-stem, ground stem, light stem and simple active stem. It is contrasted with the other six BH stems, which are referred to as *derived stems, *binyanim or augmented stems. Joüon §§41-50; MNK §16.2; GKC §§43-50.

qamets. *n.* A long *a*-class vowel that represents the sound *a* as in *father* (ָ). Since it is a long vowel, it may appear in a closed accented syllable and an open syllable. *See also* qamets hatuph.

qamets hatuph. *n.* A short vowel that is identical in form to the long vowel *qamets* (ָ). While the long *qamets* form is a long *a* sound, the *qamets hatuph* is considered a short vowel and has an *o* sound as in *top.* The only way to distinguish them is by syllabary rules and accent. The *qamets hatuph* is a short vowel and thus can appear only in a closed unaccented syllable. *See also* qamets.

qamets rachabh. *n.* An early Hebrew grammatical term for *long *qamets* to distinguish it from the *qamets hatuph*. *See also* qamets.

qatal conjugation. *See* perfect.

qatel pattern. *n.* A morphemic pattern that is adjectival and verbal in function and expresses *stative qualities. It is used with BH roots to form adjectives. For example, the root יָבֵשׁ, "to dry," plus the *qatel* pattern equals יָבֵשׁ, "dry." The pattern is also used to form verbs.

qatil pattern. *n.* A BH vowel pattern primarily used to form adjectives and substantives (e.g., נָגִיד, "leader").

qatol pattern. *n.* A BH vowel pattern that tends to express stative qualities (e.g., קָטֹן, "small").

qenemlui letters. *n.* An acronym for the six BH letters (ק, נ, מ, ל, ו, י) that in some cases drop their doubling quality *(dagesh forte)* because of being followed by a *vocal *shewa*.

Qere. *n.* "to be read." Words that in the reading of the MT are to be substituted in place of recognized scribal errors; words that are offensive and the Tetragrammaton. Joüon §16e; MNK §9.7; GKC §17. *See also* Kethib; Qere *perpetuum*.

Qere perpetuum. *n.* Certain Qere that are to be recognized permanently, such as reading the Tetragrammaton as *Adonai* because ancient Rabbinic scholars considered it too holy to be pronounced. Joüon §16e; MNK §9.7; GKC §17.

qibbuts. *n.* The masoretic representation of the *u* sound as pronounced in the English word *pull* (ֻ).

qinah meter. *n.* A metrical pattern proposed for BH poetry that characteristically has three accents in the first line and two accents in the second (3 + 2). Today the notion of meter in BH poetry is generally rejected, and the idea of *qinah* meter is widely rejected by BH scholars. *See also* meter.

Qoheleth. *n.* The Hebrew name for the book of Ecclesiastes.

qotel pattern. *n.* A common morphemic pattern in BH used to create both nouns and participles (שֹׁבֵר, "one who breaks," or "breaking"). Some are *deverbative nouns, which probably began as participles and were eventually recognized as a noun (רֹאֶה, "vision"), while others still are plain *denominatives for which no verbal root can be located (כֹּהֵן, "priest"). *See also qatal* pattern.

quadriliteral root. *n.* A stem made up of four root letters. Quadriliterals may be the result of a contraction in joining two triliteral roots but most often from the simple addition of a fourth stem letter for one of various reasons. Joüon §§60, 88; GKC §§30, 56. *See also* biliteral root; triliteral root; quinquiliteral root.

qualifier. *See* modifier.

quantifier. *See* focus particle.

quasi-ergative. *See* reflexive.

quasi-stative verbs. *See* ingressive(s).

quasi-verbal indicators. *See* particle of existence; particle of nonexistence.

quasi-verbal nominal clause. *See* existential clause.

quatrain. *n.* A poetic strophe of four lines in BH poetry.

queclarative. *adj.* Of an utterance composed in the form of a question but carrying the force of a statement.

quiescence. *n.* The case of a letter becoming silent in the pronunciation of the word but not being dropped from the *orthography. *See also* quiescent letters.

quiescent *aleph.* *n.* The tendency of *aleph* to be silent (unpronounced) while still being a root consonant of a word. In such cases it is easily mistaken for a *mater lectionis*. The quiescent *aleph* is identified in the MT by having no vowel pointing of its own (e.g., רֹאשׁ).

quiescent letters. *n.* Four Hebrew letters that were added to the text during both the preexilic and the intertestamental periods as a rudimentary form of vowel representation and in such use lost their consonantal nature and became silent: *aleph, he, waw* and *yod*. Three of these *(yod, waw, he)* are also referred to as *matres lectionis*, "mothers of reading."

quiescent *shewa.* *See* silent shewa.

quinquiliteral root. *n.* A Hebrew root that has five root consonants, a rare occurrence. *See also* biliteral root; triliteral root; quadriliteral root.

quotative frame. *n.* A single or multiple verb construction marking the end of narration and introducing a quote. In Hebrew, the most common examples are וַיֹּאמֶר, "and he said," and לֵאמֹר (the infinitive construct with *lamed* preposition), "saying."

Qumran. *n.* The location on the northwest shore of the Dead Sea where the Dead Sea Scrolls were found by an Arab shepherd boy. In subsequent excavations, an entire library was discovered in which at least a portion of every book of the BH, with the exception of Esther, was found, as well as many other commentaries and manuals. Among the ruins were found a massive graveyard and a building complex. The great *Isaiah Scroll stands out among the finds because of its near perfect state of preservation. The finds at Qumran were revolutionary for text criticism of the Hebrew Bible because they are the most complete and oldest *extant material of the Hebrew Bible. As many as five differing textual traditions, including a *protomasoretic tradition, were found there.

R

Rabbinic Hebrew. *See* Mishnaic Hebrew.

radix. Lat. "base, foundation." —*n.* A term used by medieval Christian Hebrew grammarians to refer to the stem commonly referred to as the שֹׁרֶשׁ, "root," by medieval Jewish Hebrew grammarians. *See also* stem.

raphe. n. A *masoretic accentual sign represented as a short horizontal stroke placed over a consonant and used in one of three ways. (1) Sometimes a word loses its *dagesh forte*, so *raphe* is placed above the letter to mark this change. (2) *Raphe* may also be placed over a *begadkepat* letter that has lost its *dagesh lene* in order to indicate clearly its *fricative value. (3) *Raphe* may be placed over a *word-final ה to indicate the opposite of *mappiq*, that it is vocalic in function. Joüon §12; GKC §14. *See also* external points.

real condition. *n.* A state or condition referred to in a conditional sentence that is already manifest, has taken place or is presented with a substantial surety of its fruition. Such conditions are most commonly introduced by כִּי or אִם (e.g., Gen 2:17b: כִּי בְּיוֹם אֲכָלְךָ מִמֶּנּוּ מוֹת תָּמוּת, "*for in the day you eat of it* you shall most definitely die"). *See also* unreal condition.

recension. *n.* A reworked or edited edition of a manuscript.

reciprocal. *n.* The verbal *voice that expresses mutual action. It is characterized by two or more subjects that simultaneously act upon each other, such as in "John and Marie argued with each other." It is to be contrasted with the *reflexive, in which the subject acts upon itself, and the *tolerative, in which the agent is acted upon (passive).

reciprocal pronoun. *n.* An *anaphoric element that describes a mutuality between two parties. Reciprocal pronouns support compound subjects that act upon each other (e.g., "each other," "one another"). In BH, the word אִישׁ sometimes is used with the force of a reciprocal pronoun (e.g., Gen 13:11: וַיִּפָּרְדוּ אִישׁ מֵעַל אָחִיו, "and they [Abraham and Lot] separated from *each other*").

recitativum. *n.* A conjunction or construction that is used to introduce a quotation. *See also* quotative frame.

rectum. See governing element.

redaction. *n.* The editing of a manuscript.

redaction criticism. *n.* A critical approach to the Gospels or various Old Testament books that seeks to identify the author's or editor's use of various religious traditions as well as how and why he shaped them into the canonical compositions that exist today. It is in many ways a corrective to *form criticism, which tried to look behind the text to identify the historical context of each story or tradition. Redaction criticism is less concerned with identifying the *form and *Sitz im Leben* of a text and more concerned with why the tradition was included and why it was shaped into its extant form.

redactor. *n.* Used variously in biblical criticism, especially *redaction criticism, for a scribe who edited existing traditions into a reshaped canonical form; an editor.

Redaktionsgeschichte. See redaction criticism.

reduction. *See* propretonic reduction.

redundancy. *See* pleonasm.

reduplication. *n.* The reduplication of a *biliteral root or the last two letters of a *triliteral root in the formation of another word. This is common in Aramaic. For example, the root adjective רַב, "great, chief," is reduplicated to form the word for "noble, lord," רַבְרְבָן.

referent. *n.* In theoretical linguistics, an objective thing itself. The referent is contrasted with the sign, which is the word used to denote an object or concept of some sort. The referent may be either an *animate, *inanimate or *abstract noun. The words *car* and *automobile* are both signs used in the English language system to refer to a particular referent, a machine designed for transportation.

referential. *See* denotation.

reflexive. *n.* A verbal expression in which the subject acts upon itself. The subject and the object are the same entity, such as in "I will strengthen myself." In BH, the reflexive idea is expressed mostly by the *Hithpael but also the *Niphal. *See also* reciprocal; tolerative.

reflexive pronoun. *n.* A pronoun with a reflexive force, such as English *himself, herself* or *myself*. There are no formal reflexive pronouns in BH, but the regular pronouns can be used in a reflexive sense. *See also* Hithpael stem.

regens. See governing element.

regressive assimilation. *n.* The influence of one letter upon the preceding letter to become like itself. It is more common than *progressive assimilation. For example, the syllable *im-* in the English word *immediate* is the result of a regressive assimilation. The alveolar nasal continuant *n* of the original prefix *in-* was conformed to a bilabial nasal continuant *m*. *See also* progressive assimilation; dissimilation.

regular verb. *See* strong verb.

rejection. *n.* The deletion of a *root letter from a word in inflection. When this occurs at the beginning of a word, it is called *aphaeresis. In the middle of a word, it is known as *syncope, and at the end of a word it is called *apocope.

relative clause. *n.* A subordinate clause that is introduced by a *relative pronoun (*who, which, what,* etc.). BH grammarians sometimes distinguish between the *dependent or attributive relative particles and the so-called *independent relative particles. The dependent relative refers to the use of a relative particle in a relative clause. This functions in an attributive sense to the *head word it modifies (e.g., Gen 15:7: אֲנִי יְהוָה אֲשֶׁר הוֹצֵאתִיךָ, "I am YHWH [he] who brought you out." Here the relative particle points to the head word *YHWH*. *Independent relative clauses use the relative as an object and do not have an antecedent. Joüon §158; GKC §155. *See also* relative pronoun.

relative pronoun. *n.* A pronoun that expresses relation or relates one thing to another (*who, whom, which, whose,* etc.). In BH, relative pronouns are all generally expressed by the indeclinable particle אֲשֶׁר.

Also common in BH Poetry and Mishnaic Hebrew is a shortened form (שֶׁ) that is prefixed to the word it relates. Joüon §§38, 145; MNK §36.3; GKC §§36, 138; *IBHS* §19.

Religionsgeschichte. Germ. "history of religions." —*n.* A higher-critical discipline focused on the comparative study of religion; in biblical criticism, especially a purely descriptive study of the religion of ancient Israel. It is to be contrasted with theology that is prescriptive and constructive.

Religionsgeschichtliche Schule. Germ. "history of religions school." —*n.* See *Religionsgeschichte.*

remote demonstrative. *See* far demonstrative.

repetition. *n.* The use of redundancy of words, sounds or syntactical structures in literature for various reasons. Three of the most prominent reasons are for *emphasis, rhyme and aesthetic appeal.

repetitive parallelism. *See* climactic parallelism.

resolution. *n.* The solving or satisfying of the problem or *conflict of a *narrative.

restrictive conjunctions. *See* restrictive particles.

restrictive particles. *n.* A class of conjunctions that indicate restriction or limitation (e.g., BH אַךְ and רַק, "only, nothing but"). *See also* exclusive coordination; inclusive coordination.

restrictive sentences. *See* exclusive coordination.

result clause. *n.* A subordinate clause that expresses the consequences (results) of the *main clause (e.g., Num 23:19: לֹא אִישׁ אֵל וִיכַזֵּב, "God is not a man that he should lie"). GKC §166.

resultative. *adj.* Pertaining to verbs that indicate an action terminating in a quasi-state of being. They emphasize the results of an action. In BH, the Qal stem emphasizes movement or action, while the *factitive stems emphasize resulting condition.

resumptive adverb. *See* resumptive element.

resumptive element. *n.* A grammatical element that connects a clause to the preceding subject or *casus pendens.* Resumptive elements include resumptive pronouns and resumptive adverbs that resume focus upon the previous noun. They are fairly common in BH and quite common BA (e.g., Gen 17:15: שָׂרַי אִשְׁתְּךָ לֹא־תִקְרָא אֶת־שְׁמָהּ שָׂרָי, "As for Sarai your wife, you shall not call *her* name Sarai" NASB).

retreat. *See* nesigah.

retrospective element. *See* anaphora.

reversed *nun*. *See* inverted *nun*.

reversive. *See* conversive.

rhetoric. *n.* The study and use of language for persuasive speech.

rhetorical criticism. *n.* A supplementary discipline to *form criticism that studies the literary devices and structures a particular
author uses to convey his or her thoughts within the form (genre)
being used.

rhyme. *n.* A repetition of a sound at the end of a word, *hemistich or
poetic *strophe for aesthetic appeal.

rhythm. *See* meter.

rib **pattern.** *See* covenant lawsuit.

root. *n.* A *free morpheme that is the basic form of a word after all
*bound morphemes are extracted. Among medieval Hebrew
grammarians the root was referred to as a *shoresh* (שֹׁרֶשׁ, "root").
The Northwest Semitic family of languages are characteristically
known for their *triliteral roots; however, there are a certain number of *biconsonantal and quadriconsonantal roots and even in
rare cases monoconsonantal and quinquiconsonantal roots. For
example, the root שבר is used with various stem patterns to create
a number of words, such as שָׁבוּר, "what is broken"; שֶׁבֶר, "a
crash"; מַשְׁבֵּר, "breach"; or מִשְׁבָּר, "a sea breaker." GKC §30.

root verb. *See* strong verb.

rounded vowel. *n.* Any vowel (usually a *back vowel) in which the
lips must be rounded in order to pronounce it, such as *o* or *u*. *See
also* front vowel; back vowel.

royal plural. *See* plural of majesty.

S

salvation history. *See Heilsgeschichte.*

Samaritan Pentateuch. *n.* The pentateuchal tradition of the Samaritan community at Nablus (ancient Shechem). It is used in text criticism but evidences approximately six thousand differences from
the MT. *See also* Abisha Scroll.

sapential. *adj.* Having the attributes of wisdom writing or, more
technically, of the biblical genre of wisdom literature, such as *Qoheleth, Proverbs or Job.

sarcasm. *n.* Bitter and cutting remarks with an intent to taunt or deride.

satire. *n.* A literary genre of communication characterized by sarcasm and mockery. Satire in the Hebrew Bible can be observed in Elijah's contest with the prophets of Baal in 1 Kings 18 or in Isaiah 14.

scene. *See* episode.

schema etymologicum. See cognate accusative.

scheme. *See* figurative language.

scriptio continua. n. The ancient practice of producing linear alphabetic inscriptions with no spaces between the words. *See also* word divider.

scriptio defectivus. See defective writing.

scriptio plena. See full writing.

sebir. n. סביר, "to suppose." —*n.* An *Aramaic word inserted into many ancient manuscripts to mark a marginal note for unusual words or word usage. *pl. sebirin.*

secondary accent. *n.* A secondary stress upon a syllable in a word consisting of more than two syllables (three syllables or more). It is to receive less stress than the *primary accent. Secondary stresses in BH and BA are usually marked by a *meteg.*

secondary Hiphil. See pseudo-*Hiphil.*

seder. n. A masoretic mark (ס) in the margins of the MT to indicate the pentateuchal divisions from the Palestinian rabbinic tradition. They divided the Pentateuch into 154 or 167 readings for liturgical synagogue worship. *pl. sedarim. See also parashah.*

segholate nouns. *n.* A class of BH nouns possessing an extra *segol* as a helping vowel. In antiquity these were monosyllabic roots with case endings. When the case endings were dropped, these monosyllabic forms came to require a helping vowel for smoothing pronunciation. For example, *malku* became *malk,* which became eventually *melek.*

segol. n. A member of the masoretic vowel pointing system used to represent the *e* sound as in the English word *pet.* These vowels are used extensively in *segholate* nouns.

select (verbal). *See* valency (verbal).

semanteme. *See* lexeme.

semantic domain. *See* semantic field.

semantic field. *n.* The complete range of possible meanings that a word may take in its various possible contexts. It is the task of lexical semantics to ascertain this range. *See also* lexical semantics.

semantic pertinence. *n.* A linguistic rule that requires that, although theoretically any words may be used together, they must still be combined in a way so as to have meaning together. The rule is based on the relationship between *polysemy (multiple meanings of words) and *context, which together define how a word is used.

semantics. *n.* The disciplined study of word meaning. This is broken into two major subfields: *lexical semantics, which is the study of a word's possible meanings (semantic field); and *discourse semantics, the study of a word's meaning in a discourse context. As the field grows, the term is, however, being used more loosely, and sometimes the term is used interchangeably with *semasiology.

semasiology. *n.* (1) Used broadly, a synonym for *semantics that deals with the overall meaning of words, both in context and their general semantic field; (2) defined more narrowly, lexicology in which the semantic fields of words are studied both diachronically and synchronically. *See also* diachronic linguistics; synchronic linguistics.

sememe. *n.* Used variously; a simple unit of meaning or a symbol (word).

semiagglutinating. *adj.* Relating to a language that demonstrates partial characteristics of agglutination. *See also* agglutinative language.

semiconsonant. *See* glide.

semiology. *See* semiotics

semiotic entities. *n.* The signs in a language system that are used to represent things referred to, namely, words. When meaning is attached to the signs, they become semantic entities. In modern linguistics, words have meaning or sharpened meaning in relation to one another. Consequently, when these entities (words) are placed in sentences and discourse, their meaning is further enhanced as a semantic entity.

semiotics. *n.* The scientific study of signs (Gk. *sēmeion*, "sign") of communication, the speech sounds used to refer to objects and concepts. Alphabetic writing as well as syllabic cuneiform are examples of written semiotic systems. Semiotics may be further subdivided into two subclasses: *semantics and *pragmatics.

Semitic languages. *n.* A broad classification of languages with common characteristics that are situated in the Middle East (ancient Near East), what is now known as Western Asia, and that are of the Afroasiatic language *phylum. These have in common characteristics such as phonology, morphology, vocabulary, grammar and syntax. The Semitic family of languages is broadly divided into three major groups: East Semitic (Assyrian, Babylonian), West Semitic (e.g., BH, Ugaritic, Phoenician) and South Semitic (Arabic).

Semitism. *n.* The occurrence of a word, idiom or expression in a text that evidences Semitic language influence. The Septuagint is known for *Hebraisms, and the New Testament evidences both Hebraisms and *Aramaisms.

Semito-Hamitic Languages. *See* Afroasiatic.

semivowel. *n.* A consonant (e.g., *y* or *j*) that occasionally takes on characteristics of a vowel, such as the *y* in the word *many*.

sentence. *n.* A group of words expressing a complete thought consisting of at least a subject and a predicate. The sentence is the largest unit targeted for grammatical analysis. Above it are discourse and genre. There are four basic types of sentences: declarative (makes a statement of fact); interrogative (asks a question); imperative (makes a command); and exclamatory (expresses a strong sentiment or emotion).

sentence sense. *n.* A classification of what a particular sentence is communicating. This may be contrasted with literary sense or word-level sense.

sentence stress. *See* pause.

separable preposition. *n.* A preposition that may stand alone as an independent word (*free morpheme). Separable prepositions are often joined to the word they modify by a *maqqeph, which causes *proclisis. *See also* inseparable preposition.

Sephardic. *adj.* Relating to the Hebrew pronunciation system from the Sephardim, the Jews of Spain and Portugal. It is the pronunciation used in modern Israeli. *See also* Ashkenazic.

Septuagint. *n.* The Greek translation of the Hebrew Bible that was used by Jews of the Diaspora and became the canonical text, over the Hebrew Bible, in the early church; abbr. LXX.

servi. See conjunctive accent.

serviles. *See* formative letters.

setumah. n. A *samek* (ס) inserted into the MT to mark the closing of a "closed" paragraph where the next paragraph may begin on the same line, or if space is limited, on the line immediately following. May be contrasted with **petucha* marking the closing of an "open" paragraph where traditionally a full line space intervened between paragraphs; however, **BHS is not consistent.

Shaphel. *n.* The **Aramaic *causative stem marked by the *shin* *preformative. Its function is for all practical purposes identical to the *Haphel stem. It also occurs in Mishnaic Hebrew, *Syriac and rarely in BH.

sharpened syllable. *n.* A syllable that begins with the doubled letter of the previous closed syllable. For example, the word אִמִּי is formed of two syllables (מִּי and אִ); the second is מִּי, which is the sharpened syllable. *See also* closed syllable.

sharpening. *See* doubling.

Shema. Refers to Deut 6:4 which holds the place of one of the most important liturgical and creedal texts of ancient Israel and Judaism.

Shemitic. *See* Semitic languages.

sheva. See silent *shewa*; vocal *shewa*.

shewa. n. A Masoretic pointing symbol with a variety of forms and uses, which is placed under a consonant and looks similar to a colon. The two most basic forms are *silent *shewa* and *vocal *shewa*. The vocal *shewa* has the phonetic value of a hurried or slighted *e* sound and must always precede another full vowel to form a syllable. The silent *shewa* has no phonetic value but simply acts as a syllable closer for *closed syllables (CVC). Therefore, it is placed under the second consonant of a closed syllable and always follows a preceding full vowel. One may also distinguish between a simple *shewa* and a *compound *shewa* or **hateph* vowel. Both the silent and vocal *shewa* are classed as a "simple" *shewa*. The compound *shewa* is in form the combination of a simple *shewa* followed by either a *segol, *patach* or *qamets. The compounds are also considered "vocal" and present a hurried or slighted pronunciation but more like their full vowel counterparts. Therefore, like the simple vocal *shewa*, the compound *shewa* cannot stand alone to form a syllable but must accompany a full vowel. See silent *shewa;* vocal *shewa.*

shewa mobile. *See* vocal shewa.

shewa quiescens. *See* silent *shewa.*

shewa rule. *n.* A rule specifying that when two simple *shewa*s occur at the beginning of a word, the first one becomes a *hireq* (e.g., שְׁמוּאֵל + לְ becomes לִשְׁמוּאֵל).

shewa simplex. *See* simple *shewa.*

shin causative. *See* Shaphel.

shoresh. *See* root.

short form. *See* apocope, apocopation.

short imperfect. *n.* In BA, the use of the *imperfect conjugation without the *energic *nun*, primarily in *modal expressions. It should be noted that in the majority of cases this does not differ in form from the regular imperfect, and only in special cases does an actual shortening of the form take place.

short syllable. *n.* A syllable with a consonant and a short vowel. BH syllabic value is divided into short syllables and *long syllables. A short syllable can only be an open syllable (CV) with a short vowel; open syllables with *long vowels and *closed syllables are *long syllables.

short yiqtol. *n.* The *prefix conjugation with the *waw*-consecutive (*wayyiqtol) when it denotes a simple action (not iterative or customary as *long yiqtol* indicates). *See also* long *yiqtol.*

shureq. *n.* A masoretic vowel pointing symbol (וּ) that represents the *u* sound as found in the English word *rule.* The sound was represented prior to the masoretic system by simply the *mater lectionis* vowel letter *waw.* In the masoretic system, a *dagesh was simply added to a *waw* to represent the *u* sound. *See also* qibbuts.

sibilant. *n.* A phoneme that produces some sort of *s* or hissing *fricative sound. Sibilants are pronounced with the tongue against the back of the teeth by forcing air through the teeth. BH and BA examples of sibilants are שׂ, שׁ, ס, ז and צ. Joüon §5m. *See also* affricate.

sigla. *n.* Signs and symbols used in text-critical studies to indicate various ideas and concepts. *sing.* siglum.

sign. *n.* Any linguistic element (spoken or written) that signifies an extralinguistic entity. *See also* signification.

sign of the definite direct object. See direct object marker.

significant. Fr. "what signifies." *See* signification.

signification. *n.* In modern linguistics as developed by Ferdinand de Saussure, the representation of thoughts, objects and ideas through representative signs, namely, words. Words are signs used in a language system (sign system) to signify and communicate. De Saussure distinguished between the *signified (Fr. *signifié*), which was the thought, object or idea being communicated, and the *signifier (Fr. *signifiant*), that which represents the thought, object or idea in the language system. For example, in "He has a brand new car," the signified is the automobile referred to, and the signifier is the word *car.* The same distinction is also called *sign* versus *referent* and *word* versus *concept* by theoretical linguists. Theoretically, a concept may be referred to by multiple signs, and a sign may be used to refer to multiple objects or concepts. These differences are changed by their syntagmatic relations in various *utterances.

signifié. Fr. "what is signified." *See* signification.

signified. *See* signification.

signifier. *See* signification.

silent *shewa.* The masoretic sign ( ) that marks a closed syllable (CVC); also called a syllable divider. It is identical in form to *vocal *shewa.* A *shewa* is silent when (1) it is the first of two in a row; (2) after an unaccented short vowel; and (3) with final *kaph.* Joüon §8; MNK §8.1; GKC §10. *See also* compound *shewa.*

silluq. *n.* A masoretic textual accent represented by a short vertical stroke under the accented syllable of a word ( ). It is only found under the last word of a Hebrew verse and marks a word in *pause. *See also* meteg.

Siloam Inscription. An important inscription written in classical Hebrew prose dating to the reign of King Hezekiah of Judah in the seventh to sixth centuries B.C. It was carved in the lower entrance to what is called Hezekiah's tunnel in what is now the Arab village of Silwan south of the temple mount in Jerusalem. The tunnel served as a water conduit for Jerusalem during the siege of the Assyrian Monarch Sennacharib, according to 2 Kings 20:20 and 2 Chronicles 32:30. The inscription's content celebrates the success of the quarrymen. It was discovered in about 1880 and was illicitly removed and broken and now resides in the Museum of the Ancient Orient in

Istanbul.

simile. *n.* The characterization of one thing by likening it to something else. It is always marked with a preposition such as *like* or *as*. It is usually accomplished in BH by use of the prefixed preposition בְּ. *See also* metaphor.

simple active. *See* Qal stem.

simple passive. *See* Niphal stem.

simple pattern. *See* vowel patterns.

simple plosion (*dagesh* of). *See* plosion.

simple sentence. *n.* An independent clause composed of just a subject and a predicate.

simple *shewa*. *n.* The simple form of the *shewa* in both its *silent* or *vocal* functions (ְ). Simple *shewa* is to be contrasted with complex or *compound *shewa*.

simple syllable. *See* open syllable.

simple *waw*. See *waw*-conjunctive.

simple word. *n.* In linguistic terminology, a single morphological unit that can stand alone. A simple word is a word in its most basic form with no *prefixes, *suffixes or *infixes attached. For example, the word *boy* is a simple word because it can be broken down no further, in contrast to *boys*, which is a complex word that may be broken down into *boy* (lexeme) and *s* (plural sufformative).

Sinai Script. *n.* Among the earliest alphabetic scripts located at the mines of Serabit el-Khadem in southern Sinai; the script was acrophonic. *See also* acrophony.

singular. *adj.* Denoting one of someone or something. Deviations from simple singular understandings are *collective nouns and *plurale tantum*. MNK §24.3; *IBHS* §7.2.

singularia tantum. *n.* Words that occur only in a singular form, such as *collective nouns.

singulative. *n.* A noun that, although it may be *marked plural, is intrinsically singular or used to refer to a collective body as a whole; also referred to as *nomen unitatis* (e.g., שָׁמַיִם, "heavens"). Collective nouns may also be unmarked and have a marked singulative counterpart. For example, the collective אֳנִי, "fleet," has its singulative counterpart אֳנִיָּה, "a ship."

Sitz im Leben. Germ. "setting in life." —*n.* A technical term of criticism in general and *form criticism in particular that refers to the life setting in which events took place or the context out of which *forms or *genres grew. It was first used by Hermann Gunkel.

slot. *See* morphemic slot.

smoothing. *n.* The scribal process of smoothing out, unifying or leveling grammatical and linguistic usage. Textual transmitters at times chose to smooth out inconsistencies in grammar, pronunciation and even the use of words that may have come to be viewed as incorrect, risqué or offensive.

softening. *See* weakening.

solecism. *n.* The use of incorrect grammar or a defection from grammatical concord, sometimes purposefully. *See also* archaism; modernizing.

sonant. *n.* A letter pronounced as a *voiced *continuant that has a constant flow of air that may continue until exhausted (נ, מ, ל, ר, י, ו).

soph passuq. A masoretic mark represented by two diamond-shaped dots arranged like a colon (:) and appearing at the end of a verse in the MT text tradition to mark the verse's termination.

sortals. *See* universals.

sound laws. *n.* Rules or patterns of phonological behavior within languages. *See also* Canaanite shift.

sound shift. *n.* A phonetic sound that has occurred as a systematic change across an entire language as compared to one of its cognate languages. For instance, Aramaic has broadly used a *dalet* where Hebrew uses a *zayin*. The Canaanite dialects of the Northwest Semitic family of languages are known for the common *sound shift referred to as the *Canaanite shift.

South Arabic. *See Geʿez.*

South Semitic. *See* Southwest Semitic.

Southwest Semitic. *n.* In general terms, the entire Arabic family of Semitic languages, including *Classical Arabic as found in the *Qurʾan, modern colloquial Arabic dialects, Sabaean and Ethiopic (Geʿez).

spatial. *adj.* Designating the *locative relationship of objects to one another. The term can more specifically relate to the linguistic subdiscipline of *deictics.

speech act. *See* performative utterance.

speech-act theory. *n.* In linguistic philosophy, the consideration of the capacity of language to perform acts (e.g., to make a pledge, to forgive). *See also* performative utterance.

spirant. *n.* A letter that is pronounced without any full restriction to the airflow. The *begadkepat* letters are considered to be spirants (aspirated) when the *dagesh lene* is dropped. The aspirated forms are ב, ג, ד, כ, פ and ת. Spirants are also classed as *continuants.

spirantization. *n.* A softening in the pronunciation of a hard consonant. In BH and BA this takes place in the *begadkepat* letters when they are immediately preceded by a vowel. It is primarily indicated by the dropping of the *dagesh lene* and supplementally indicated by the use of a *raphe*. Joüon §19; MNK §4.2; GKC §21. *See also* spirant.

split object. *See* split phrase.

split phrase. *n.* A syntagm that has been split in two by an intervening sentence element. In such cases, a part of the sentence intervenes between the subject or object and some adjectival (e.g., Ruth 1:1 וַיֵּלֶךְ אִישׁ מִבֵּית־לֶחֶם יְהוּדָה לָגוּר בִּשְׂדֵי מוֹאָב הוּא וְאִשְׁתּוֹ וּשְׁנֵי בָנָיו: "And *a certain man went from Bethlehem of Judah* to sojourn in the fields of Moab, *he, his wife, and his two sons*").

split subject. *See* split phrase.

spontaneous gemination. *n.* The doubling of a consonant that does not have any intrinsic cause (such as a *factitive verbal stem) or extrinsic cause (such as *assimilation) to explain its existence; an arbitrary occurrence of gemination that probably grew out of the evolution of the language. Joüon §§18c, 20c.

square character script. *n.* The alphabetic script used in the Hebrew Bible and in later Hebrew documents such as the Mishnah and Talmud and also in Aramaic documents; also called the block script or Assyrian character script. This was a later adaptation from Aramaic and is broadly used among the Dead Sea manuscripts.

stairlike parallelism. *See* climactic parallelism.

stanza. *See* strophe.

static verb. *See* stative verb.

stative verb. *n.* A verb that describes a state of being rather than an action involving motion (e.g., "I *am* strong"). In BH there are two classes of stative verbs: those marked by a *tsere* in the second syllable (e.g., כָּבֵד) and those marked by a *holem* in the second syllable (e.g., קָטֹן). There are also two classes of stative verbs in BA:

those marked with an *hireq* in the final syllable (e.g., סָגַד.) and those marked by a *tsere* in the final syllable (e.g., קָרֵב.). *See also* fientive verb.

status absolutus. *See* absolute state.

status constructus. *See* construct state.

stela. *n.* A stone pillar or monument erected in the ancient Near East for the commemoration of a significant person or event, often related to a particular monarch and his acts of diplomacy or military campaigns. *pl.* stelae. *See also* Mesha Stela.

stem. *n.* (1) Used generally, the word to which other *bound morphemes are attached; (2) in BH, a synonym for the *root word or the vowel *patterns that are added to the consonantal roots in inflection. GKC §30. *See also* verb stem.

stem consonant. *n.* Any of the letters of a Semitic *root or *stem; also called formative letters. Stem consonants are to be contrasted with preformative consonants, which arise by morphology.

stem vowel. *See* characteristic vowel.

stich. *n.* A single line of poetic verse; a synonym for a *colon or *hemistich. The term is sometimes used synonymously for distich and bicolon as well.

stop. *n.* A consonant in which the flow of air must be completely stopped in order to pronounce it. *See also* plosive.

strengthening. *See* doubling.

strong disjunction. *See* disjunctive.

strong verb. *n.* A verb that acts according to the regular inflectional patterns; also referred to as a regular verb. In BH, strong verbs are characterized primarily by the static nature of the three root consonants, in contrast to *weak verbs.

strong *waw.* *See* waw-consecutive.

strophe. *n.* A grouping of poetic verses consisting of two or more *cola that possesses metrical unity. While bearing many accidental characteristics such as rhyme, *meter and accentuation, a strophe is mostly unified around a theme to which all the verses work together to communicate. Lamentations is characterized by strophes constituted of two verses (*bicola) and three verses (*tricola). *See also* colon.

structural meaning. *See* structural sense.

structural pressure. *n.* The inherent conventions of language that may cause a change or sound shift in a language. It is the tendency to regularize exceptions and anomalies in language on account of certain established patterns in the language.

structural sense. *n.* The meaning a word takes on in the context of a particular sentence structure in which it appears, as contrasted with the more generalized lexical sense.

structuralism. *n.* In applied linguistics, the theory that a language is a unique system in which all the complex units gain their meaning from their relationship to other units. According to structuralists, language is a system of relations or interrelated systems. This theory can, for the most part, be attributed to the work of Ferdinand de Saussure. The structuralist, by means of descriptive analysis, seeks to determine general conceptual rules of the language to further analyze communicative utterances. Originally structuralism was primarily concerned with sentence construction and lesser units. Since then, linguists have been forced to reckon with analysis of discourses.

stylus. *n.* A sharp writing instrument used to inscribe (usually *cuneiform) on clay tablets in the ancient Near East.

subgenre. *n.* A *genre within a larger literary genre, such as the presence of law or a victory hymn written into the fabric of a *narrative, as is found in the book of Exodus.

subject. *n.* The nominal element in a clause or sentence that either commits the action of an *active verb or receives the action of a *passive verb. It is the nominal element in a clause that the *predicate describes.

subject clause. *n.* When an entire clause is employed as a subject; e.g. *"I left early,* is what he said." *See also* object clause.

subject complement. *n.* A noun in a *nominal clause that states what the subject is. *See also* predicate adjective; complement.

subject pronoun. *n.* In BH, a *free morpheme pronoun that is used as the subject of a sentence; also called an independent personal pronoun. Subject pronouns are often used in verbless clauses and for emphasis in verbal clauses. They are to be contrasted with direct-object pronouns.

subjective case. *See* nominative case.

subjective genitive. *n.* (1) A genitival noun (or pronoun) that forms part of the whole concept of the subject (e.g., Gen 15:1: דְּבַר־

יְהוָה אֶל־אַבְרָם, "The word *of* YHWH came unto Abram"); (2) a genitive relationship in which the governing noun *(regens)* indicates that the governed noun *(rectum)* possess a certain quality, state or material thing (e.g., הֵיכַל יְהוָה, "the temple of YHWH"). Joüon §129. *See also* construct state.

subjunctive mood. *n.* A *volitive mood that expresses a wish or purpose, rather than a concrete action, with a relative possibility of fruition. It should be contrasted with the *optative, which expresses a wish or purpose with unlikely chances of fruition. This distinction is not consistently recognized, however, and many use the terms interchangeably.

sublinear. *adj.* Meaning below the line of writing.

subordinate clause. *n.* A clause that is in a necessary relationship to an independent (main) clause. Subordinate clauses are also referred to as dependent clauses because they depend upon the independent clause to make sense. In "He was singing while he was walking," for example, "while he was walking" is a subordinate clause because it cannot stand alone.

subordinating conjunction. *See* conjunction.

substantival clause. *n.* Any clause that by itself may act as either a subject (*subjective substantive) or an object (*objective substantive). For example, in תּוֹעֵבָה יִבְחַר בָּכֶם, "He who chooses you is an abomination" (Is 41:24), the verbal clause "he who chooses you" functions as a predicate nominative in a nominal clause. Joüon §157. *See also* object clause.

substantive. *n.* (1) Narrowly, an independent noun in contrast to a dependent noun (adjective); (2) broadly, any part of speech used as a noun, such as a participle, gerund (e.g., "*Running* is good exercise"), infinitive (e.g., "*To exercise* is good for health"), adjective, phrase, or even, in some cases, an entire sentence.

subtext. *n.* A discrete text within a larger text or literary body.

subtextual. *adj.* Relating to a theme or idea in a composition conveyed in implicit terms and not forthrightly stated.

suffix. *n.* A bound morpheme added to the end of a word to modify its meaning in some way; also called a sufformative.

suffix conjugation. *See* perfect conjugation.

suffixes of connection. *n.* The somewhat inexplicable use of *-i* and *-o* suffixes attached to some words in construct. The second of the two is rare, but the first is common in BH poetry, most often attached to a *nominative noun.

sufformative. *See* suffix.

Sumerian. *n.* The ancient language (non-Semitic) of the Sumerian peoples of southern Mesopotamia in the fourth through third millennia. The Sumerians developed *cuneiform writing, which evolved in their culture from early *pictograms and *logograms. Eventually Sumerian was succeeded in Mesopotamia by Akkadian, which adopted the cuneiform writing system.

superfluous. *n.* Any unneeded sentence element. Some grammarians observe the so-called superfluous *waw* (2 Sam 13:20).

superlative. *adj.* Of any unit of communication that establishes something as superior to all others. *See also* superlative degree.

superlative degree. *n.* A level of comparative degree in which one thing is expressed as being superior to all others. In English it is expressed by the sufformative *-est* (e.g., the biggest). In BH it is expressed in more than one way, but one of the most common methods is by binding the singular *construct form of a noun to its *absolute plural *cognate, forming a cognate genitive relationship (e.g., שִׁיר הַשִּׁירִים, "Song of songs"; מֶלֶךְ מְלָכִים, "King of kings"). It may also be expressed by use of the article (e.g., הַגָּדוֹל, "the greatest") or by using מְאֹד following the adjective (e.g., טוֹב מְאֹד, "best"). Joüon §141; MNK §30.5; GKC §133; *IBHS* §14.5. *See also* degree; comparative degree; positive degree.

superordinate. *n.* In semantics, a word that holds the place of a larger grouping or category into which hyponyms fall. For example, *fruit* is a superordinate to *apple* and *orange*, which are classed as *hyponyms to *fruit*.

supplement clause. *n.* A clause that functions in an adjunctive capacity to that of the main clause. It is considered *omissible and thus adds supplementary information to the sentence without which the main clause would still make sense. It is contrasted with a *complement clause, which is necessary for completing the thought of the sentence.

suppletive verbs. *See* defective verbs.

supralinear. *adj.* Meaning written above the line of writing.

suprasegmental. *adj.* Relating to aspects of communication that assist meaning but that are not words in and of themselves, such as pitch, stress and intonation.

suprasentential. *adj.* In structural linguistics, referring to the analysis of language and its relations above the sentence level. One might study how the structure of a discourse contributes to the overall meaning or how various words throughout the discourse serve to define and refine one another's meaning.

surface structure. *n.* In transformational grammar, surface structure (also called S-structure), is the syntactical interrelationship of words in forming a particular sentence. It is to be contrasted with the *deep structure, which is focused upon the essence of the idea conveyed and is arrived at by a series of grammatical transformations. Theoretically, two sentences could have the same surface structure and a different deep structure and so on.

surrogate. *n.* Any element that is used in place of something else. Pronouns are surrogates for the nouns they replace.

suspended case. *See casus pendens.*

suspended letters. *n.* Letters in the MT that were purposely written higher than the rest (supralinear) for various scribal reasons (e.g., Judg 18:30).

suzerainty treaty. *See* treaty.

syllabary. *n.* A glossary of syllabic signs for the representation of words. Earlier Semitic languages and Sumerian were written in a *syllabic writing system.

syllabic constitution. *n.* The analysis of how syllables are formed in general. In Semitic syllable constitution, two major governing principles determine the vowel quality (long or short) and the syllable classification (open or closed). This provides for a number of combinations. An *open syllable is a consonant followed by a vowel (CV). A *closed syllable is composed of a consonant followed by a vowel and then by a consonant (CVC). A syllable is considered long if it is an open syllable with a *long vowel or a closed syllable. Thus, a closed syllable is considered long by default even if its vowel is short. When a closed syllable possesses a long vowel, it is sometimes referred to as an *ultralong syllable.

syllabic cuneiform. *See* cuneiform.

syllabic writing. *n.* A form of writing that represents individual syllables rather than individual letter sounds. Akkadian, Babylonian and Sumerian were written in a syllabic *cuneiform (wedge-shaped writing).

syllabification. *n.* The rules that govern the *syllabic constitution of a given language.

syllable. *See* syllabic constitution.

syllable closer. *See* silent shewa.

syllable divider. *See* silent shewa.

syllepsis (of verbal person). *n.* The agreement of a verb's indication of person with the *pronominal suffixes of a noun rather than with the construct noun itself (e.g., Is 26:9: נַפְשִׁי אִוִּיתִיךָ בַלַּיְלָה אַף־רוּחִי בְקִרְבִּי אֲשַׁחֲרֶךָ, "My soul, *I long* for you in the night; indeed, my spirit within me, *I desire* you"). Joüon §151.

Symmachus. *n.* A second-century A.D. translation of the Hebrew Bible into Greek by an Ebionite Christian of the same name. It was reliant upon the *Septuagint, *Aquila and *Theodotion.

synchronic linguistics. *n.* A linguistic study approach that focuses primarily on the form and function of a language at a particular point in time. *See also* diachronic linguistics.

syncopation. *n.* (1) On the level of vowels, the reduction of a full vowel to that of a silent *shewa*; (2) on the consonantal level, the shortening of a word by the dropping of a consonant in the middle of the word (e.g., מְאוּם becomes מוּם). Syncope is common in verbal stems with *he* preformatives in the *prefix conjugation. For example, the *Hiphil imperfect of קטל drops the expected ה and becomes יַקְטִיל. Joüon §17e. *See also* apocope; aphaeresis.

syncope. *n.* The absence of a phoneme. *See* syncopation.

synecdoche. *n.* A figure of speech using a general for a particular. For example, "The *United States* won the ice hockey!" means that the United States *hockey team* won the Olympic hockey tournament.

syndeton. *n.* The linking of phrases or clauses (*syntagms) by means of a conjunction. Syndetic constructions are to be contrasted with *asyndetic constructions. Joüon §177.

synonymous parallelism. *n.* In BH, a *bicola poetic structure in which the B colon repeats the same theme as in the A colon. *See also* antithetic parallelism; chiastic sentence; emblematic parallelism; climactic parallelism; synthetic parallelism.

synonymy. *n.* The relationship of very close meaning in words. Because of polysemy (multiple meanings of words), absolute synonyms are rare. For example, the cursing of the ground in Genesis 3:17 is referred to by אָרַר, while the cursing is referred to in 8:21 by קָלַל.

syntactic parallelism. *n.* A form of literary parallelism in which the syntactical structure of various cola show similarity or equivalence.

syntactic position. *n.* One of the various roles that a noun (absolute noun in BH) can assume in a sentence, such as subject, object or indirect object; also called syntagmatic slot. *See also* syntagm.

syntagm. *n.* A word or series of words that make up a discrete bundle of meaning. They are *word groups that grammatically function as a single word. The infinitive phrase "to go away" in the sentence, "He wants the dog to go away," acts as a single discrete unit of meaning, though it is made up of three parts: the *infinitive marker (to), the verb (go) and the modifier (away). The term *syntagm* is not limited to words or word groups, however, but may also refer to *phrases, *clauses, *sentences and larger blocks of communication. In the higher levels of *syntagmatics, linguists identify so-called "syntagmatic slots" (or just "slots"). These are ordered locations in a series of words where position actually is determinative of meaning. English is a language that is predominantly reliant upon syntagmatic slots. For example, although "John hit the ball" and "The ball hit John" both employ the same structure and the identical word elements, they are radically different in meaning because of the word elements being inserted into differing slots. A prime BH example is the difference in word order between *attributive and *predicate adjectives. The former generally follow the noun they modify, and the latter usually precede the noun they modify (attributive adjective: אִישׁ טוֹב, "a good man"; predicate adjective: טוֹב הָאִישׁ, "the man is good"). Syntagms may also be referred to as syntagmemes, word chains and constituents.

syntagmatic relations. *See* syntagmatics.

syntagmatics. *n.* The study of linguistic units (syntagms) in relation to one another in sentence construction; the study of the network of relationships in a given utterance in order to understand the words in light of these relations. *See also* syntax.

syntagmeme. *See* tagmeme.

syntax. *n.* The scientific study of word usage in clause construction. Syntax considers the ordering and arrangement of words into sentences as well as the linguistic study and analysis of sentence structure.

synthetic parallelism. *n.* In BH, a *bicola poetic structure in which the B colon furthers or intensifies the thought of the A colon. *See also* antithetic parallelism; chiastic sentence; emblematic parallelism; climactic parallelism; synonymous parallelism.

Syriac. *n.* A branch of *Aramaic; Syriac was spoken and used by early Christians living in Syria who translated the Old Testament and the New Testament into a Syriac version known as the *Peshitta. Syriac is still in use as a liturgical language.

systematic correspondence. *n.* The occurrence of changes (or variations) in a language in which certain sounds are replaced by others in a generally consistent manner; also referred to as Grimm's law. For instance, Proto-Semitic $\acute{g}$ remains $\acute{g}$ in Ugaritic but becomes צ in BH. Similarly, Proto-Semitic $\underline{d}$ undergoes regular changes in the various Semitic languages: Proto-Semitic $\underline{d}$ = Ugaritic $d/\check{z}$ = Aramaic d = BH z = Akkadian z = Arabic $\underline{d}$. Based on this correspondence, one can explain the relationship for the BH word for "gold" (זהב) and the Aramaic word for "gold" (דהב).

T

tagmeme. *n.* An *optional or *obligatory constituent that constitutes the fundamental unit of sentential construction; also called a syntagmeme. Tagmemes are inserted into theoretical syntagmatic *slots.

tagmemics. *n.* A linguistic approach developed by Kenneth Lee Pike and Robert E. Longacre that studies the relationship between syntagmatic slots (e.g., subject, predicate, object) and the *syntagmemes that may be inserted into those slots (e.g., noun, noun phrase, infinitive phrase, verbal phrase, etc.)

tale. *See* novella.

Talmud. *n.* The major collections of early rabbinic tradition and teaching, including the *Mishnah, Tosefta and extended commentaries surrounding them. There are two Talmudic traditions: the *oriental, from the Jewish rabbinic community of Babylon, which produced the Babylonian Talmud (Talmud Babli), and the *occidental, from Tiberius of Palestine and represented by the Palestinian Talmud (Talmud Yerushalmi). The editorial work for the former took place around 500-600 A.D. and the latter around 400-450 A.D. *See also* Amoraim; Tannaim.

Tanak. An acronym formed from the first letters of the three traditional divisions of the Hebrew canon: Torah (Law), Nebiim (Prophets) and Ketubim (Writings).

Tanakh. *See* Tanak.

Tannaim. תַנָּאִים, "repeaters [of the law]." —*n.* The early rabbinic scholars responsible for producing the *Mishnah, *Pirqe Aboth*, Tosefta and other important tractates found in the Babylonian and Palestinian *Talmuds.

tannaitic period. *n.* Approximately the first two centuries A.D. *See also* Tannaim.

target language. *n.* (1) A language that is the subject of study or communication; (2) the language into which a translation is made.

targum. Mishnaic Hebrew "translation." —*n.* An Aramaic translation produced by early rabbinic scholars for public reading of Scripture in the synagogue. Targumim were not always literal translations but often paraphrases that took some degree of interpretive liberty.

Targum Jerusalem I. See Targum Pseudo-Jonathan.

Targum Jerusalem II. See Fragmentary Targum.

Targum Jonathan. n. The official targum of the Prophets for Judaism. It probably had its origin in Palestine.

Targum Onqelos. n. The official targum of the Pentateuch for Judaism. It possibly had its origin in Babylon, but this is debated.

Targum Pseudo-Jonathan. n. A targum that is peculiar for combining material of the official *Targum Onqelos* with midrashic material; also called *Targum Jerusalem I.*

tautology. *n.* The needless repetition or redundancy in use of terms in spoken or written communication. *See also* pleonasm.

tD stem. *n.* A verbal stem of the Semitic languages that has an infixed *tav* plus a doubling of the medial root consonant. It is also referred to as the *reflexive stem and corresponds to BH *Hithpael.

telic. *adj.* Pertaining to an end or purpose.

telic clause. *See* purpose clause.

telic conjunction. *n.* A conjunction that indicates final purpose (e.g., אֲשֶׁר, "that"; לְמַעַן, "in order that"; פֶּן, "lest"; לְבִלְתִּי, "that not") and marks a *final purpose (telic) clause.

temporal. *adj.* Pertaining to a word, *clause, *phrase or *particle that relates the verbal action in time.

temporal adverb. *n.* An adverb that points to a particular time of action. Examples of BH temporal demonstratives include כִּי and כַּאֲשֶׁר, "when"; אַחֲרֵי, "after"; לְפְנֵי, "before"; and מֵאָז, "since."

temporal assertive adverb. *n.* An adverb that expresses the idea of "still" or "yet."

temporal clause. *n.* A clause with a deictic element that defines a temporal frame of reference in relation to the action of the main clause (e.g., Josh 5:13: וַיְהִי בִּהְיוֹת יְהוֹשֻׁעַ בִּירִיחוֹ וַיִּשָּׂא עֵינָיו, "*and when Joshua was near Jericho*, he lifted up his eyes"). Joüon §166; GKC §164.

temporal frame. *n.* The use of a *deictic element to place temporal limits on a situation or to mark out a specified time frame.

tense. *n.* The relationship of a verbal action to time. English is classified as having six tenses, some requiring the aid of verbal auxiliaries: (1) present (simple; "I come"); (2) future (auxiliary; "I *will* come"); (3) past (simple; "I came"); (4) present-perfect (auxiliary; "I *have* come"); (5) past-perfect (auxiliary; "I *had* come"; also called the pluperfect); and (6) future-perfect (auxiliary; "I *will have* come"). On the conjugational level, BH and most Semitic languages have only two indicative forms (the perfect and the imperfect), which convey verbal *aspect rather than tense per se. Tense in BH must be discerned from syntax and context along with verbal morphology. Joüon §§111-113; MNK §§14-15.2; GKC §§40, 106-107; *IBHS* §§29-31.

tenues. *n.* In BH, the *begadkepat* letters in their original hardened form represented by insertion of a *dagesh lene*. GKC §21.

tenuous. *adj.* Pertaining to letters that are voiceless and unaspirated. *See* tenues.

terminal letter. *n.* The last letter of a Semitic root word.

termination. *n.* Any sufformative arising in morphology. *See also* gender; number.

terminus ad quem. Lat. "limit to which." —*n.* The latest possible date for an event.

terminus ad quo. Lat. "limit from which." —*n.* The earliest possible date for an event.

terseness. *n.* A characteristic of BH verse in which the *strophes are composed with only the most essential elements.

test motif. *n.* A literary *plot motif in which the *protagonist is placed under a test. The near sacrifice of Isaac in Genesis 22 is probably the most well known in the Hebrew Bible.

Tetragrammaton. Lat. "the four letters." —*n.* The divine name יהוה. Rabbinic Judaism has traditionally considered the Tetragrammaton a *Qere *perpetuam* and thus has always read it aloud as *Adonai,* "the Lord."

Tetrateuch. *n.* An academic term designating Genesis through Numbers. *See also* Pentateuch.

text. *n.* A written document for study. In biblical studies (grammar, linguistics, theology), the term refers to the particular piece of a composition that is the object of study. A text may be understood as a *pericope or a *discourse. *See also* co-text; context.

text linguistics. *n.* The modern scientific study of linguistic communication in text form. It looks beyond syntax to discover how utterances are formed. This is done by analyzing semantic usage as well as linguistic conventions in order to understand how coherent communications are formed in any *target language.

textual criticism. *n.* The scientific historical study of ancient manuscripts and their transmission. It is also referred to as "lower criticism" and endeavors to distinguish and preserve what is "original" to texts as well as to identify *accretions.

textual variant. *See* variant

textus receptus. Lat. "received text" —*n.* (1) In Old Testament textual criticism, the second Rabbinic Bible of Jacob ben Chayyim, published A.D. 1524-1525, which provided the base text for Rudolph Kittel's *Biblia Hebraica* and other modern editions, such as *Biblia Hebraica Stuttgartensia;* (2) more generally, the Masoretic Text.

theme. *See* vowel patterns.

theme vowel. *See* characteristic vowel.

Theodotion. *n.* A late second-century A.D. translation of the Hebrew Bible into Greek (a possible recension of the LXX), attributed to a Jewish proselyte of the same name. It was widely used by the

church fathers of the third and fourth centuries and is still important to text criticism.

Tigrinya. *n.* A South Semitic language of the Ethiopic family spoken
in Northern Ethiopia.

timbre. *n.* (1) Used generically, sound distinctions; (2) in linguistics,
the distinction between various vowel qualities. Comparative
Semitics recognizes three basic proto-Semitic timbre: *a*, *i*, and *u* (as
represented in the three forms of the Ugaritic *aleph*). All other
vowel qualities are believed to be derived from these three. Joüon
§6.

tiqqune sopherim. תקוני ספרים, "scribal corrections." —*n.* According to the *Talmuds, scribal corrections of the Hebrew Bible that
were to smooth or correct offensive or objectionable-sounding material. See also *itture sopherim.*

tolerative. *adj.* Referring to a grammatical construction in which the
agent is portrayed as allowing itself to be acted upon (i.e., passive).
In such cases the agent is usually a human or, if not, something living or with personality. *See also* reflexive; reciprocal.

tone syllable. *n.* The syllable that takes the primary accent in a
word. *See also* secondary accent.

tone-long vowel. *See* heightening.

topic-comment construction. *n.* A *nominative absolute and the following sentence providing information about it.

toponym. *n.* (1) A place name; (2) a scribal *gloss that explains a certain ancient location with a contemporary name. *See also* patronym.

Torah. The Hebrew term applied to legal or instructive material in
the Pentateuch but came to be used in Judaism generally in reference to the *Pentateuch itself as the first of the three divisions of
the Hebrew canon. The term is usually translated "law" but in reality a more accurate rendering would be "instruction." *See also*
Tanak.

Tosefta. *n.* A body of post-biblical rabbinic writings that comprised
rabbinic discussions over various topics based upon the Mishnah
and the Hebrew Scriptures. The term literally means "supplement," meaning that it was supplemental to that of the Mishnah.
The Mishnah and Tosefta together provided the foundation for the
Talmuds. *See also* Mishnah; Talmud.

totality transfer. *n.* A semantic error, common with traditional word-study methods, in which the interpreter applies many or all of the possible meanings in a word's *semantic field to a single use of that word in a given context; also called illegitimate totality transfer.

tradent. *n.* In biblical criticism, an individual responsible for passing on oral traditions, especially religious traditions.

traditio. *n.* The process performed by *tradents; the preserving and passing on of religious traditions.

tradition criticism. *n.* A form of biblical criticism that studies the transmission of oral traditions. It is distinguishable from all other forms of criticism because it (for most scholars) focuses on the pre-literary stage of composition.

tradition-historical criticism. *See* tradition criticism.

Traditionsgeschichte. *See* tradition criticism.

traditum. *n.* A technical term for the actual oral and written material passed on in successive generations of a religious or sectarian community. *See also* tradent; *traditio.*

tragedy. *n.* A narrative form in which the story begins in prosperity and ends in calamity; contrast with *comedy.

transformational (generative) grammar. *See* generative grammar.

transitional *patach.* *See* furtive *patach.*

transitive verb. *n.* A verb that takes a direct object (accusative), such as "John hit *the ball.*" *See also* intransitive verb.

transliteration. *n.* The conversion of a word from one language or writing system to another language or writing system, such as writing BH מלך as English *mlk.*

transmission. *n.* The copying and preserving of a manuscript over the ages, especially *canonical material.

transparency. *n.* In the study of semantics, a clear or logical connection drawn between a word and its referent; an obvious or natural relationship between the sign and the thing signified. *See also* opacity, opaqueness; signification.

transposition. *See* metathesis.

treaty. *n.* A distinct legal and diplomatic literary form extant in many ancient Near Eastern and especially Hittite documents. The *form contains six major subsections: (1) preamble; (2) historical prologue; (3) stipulations; (4) deposit; (5) witnesses (usually divine or terrestrial); and (6) blessings and curses. Treaties may be classified into two major groupings: parity treaties, in which the contract is one of mutual consent between relative equals; and vassal treaties, in which one is a conquering suzerain and the other a conquered vassal. A great amount of work was done in the latter part of the twentieth century comparing the ancient Near Eastern treaty forms to biblical material, especially the book of the covenant (Ex 21—24) and Deuteronomy as a whole.

tricolon. *n.* A set of three cola. *See also* colon.

triconsonantal root. *See* triliteral root.

triliteral root. *n.* A root word consisting of a total of three root consonants. The triliteral root is the standard building block for Semitic words.

triptote. *n.* A system of nominal inflection using three morphological cases. For example, Ugaritic has a triptotic system consisting of nominatives represented with -*u*, genitives with -*i* and accusatives with -*a*. *See also* diptote; diptotic.

triptotic. *adj.* Pertaining to a three-case morphological system. *See also* triptote.

triradical root. *See* triliteral root.

trochaic meter. *n.* A form of metrical verse that is based upon trochees, a syllabic metrical foot in which the first syllable is accented and the second unaccented. This is opposite to *iambic meter.

trope. *See* figurative language.

tropology. *n.* An interpretational approach that seeks to discover hidden ethical and spiritual meaning behind the literal sense of a passage. *See also* midrash.

tsere. *n.* An *e*-class vowel represented by two horizontally aligned dots (ֵ) pronounced as the *e* sound in the English word *prey*. In some cases the regular *tsere* is considered to be a *defective form of *tsere-yod*. In most cases it represents a long *e* that has been lengthened from an original short *i*. Unlike *tsere-yod*, which is unchangeably long, it can be reduced to a *shewa*. *See also* pretonic reduction; propretonic reduction.

tsere-yod. *n.* An unchangeably long *e*-class vowel represented by two horizontally aligned dots and a letter *yod* (ֵי) and pronounced as the *e* sound in the English word *prey*. *Tsere-yod* (ֵי) is the *plene form of standard *tsere*; it is pronounced the same, but cannot be reduced.

type scene. *n.* A literary convention consisting of common ingredients, recognized by both narrator and audience, for relating an episode within a story. Examples in the HB are sibling rivalry, a man meeting a woman at a well and the testament of a dying hero.

typology. *n.* An interpretive approach that seeks to find in earlier texts parallel figures to clearer manifestations in latter texts. This has been a common practice over the centuries among Christian interpreters trying to find typological meaning about Christ in the events, institutions or lives of Old Testament persons. The Bible itself makes use of typologies, as when the book of Hebrews (8:5) likens the Israelite tabernacle to heavenly things. However, it has also been greatly abused by interpreters to the point of allegorizing and spiritualizing (see also 1 Cor 10:1-6; Rom 5:14; Gal 4:21-31).

U

Ugaritic. *n.* A Northwest Semitic dialect recorded on texts unearthed at Tel Ras Shamra in Northern Syria. It was the language spoken at the ancient city of Ugarit, which flourished from the Late Bronze Age to the Early Iron Age. It is considered to be an alphabetic *cuneiform script and thus must be distinguished from the *syllabic cuneiform writing systems of Mesopotamia. This alphabetic cuneiform consists of thirty letters that generally correspond to the consonantal values of other Northwest Semitic alphabetic systems. The epic poetry of Ugarit has contributed significantly to modern understandings of the *Psalter.

ultimate constituents. *n.* The most fundamental elements of sentential constructions understood as *morphemes. One identifies ultimate constituents by reducing an utterance to the morphological level, e.g., the ultimate constituents of "They were petting the friendly cat," are "they, were, pet, -ing, the, friend, -ly, cat." *See also* immediate constituents.

ultralong syllable. *n.* A closed syllable with a long vowel. In BH, *long syllables are either an *open syllable with a long vowel or a *closed syllable. When a closed syllable (CVC) has a long vowel, it is often referred to as ultralong. *See also* syllabic constitution.

unchangeable vowels. *See* unchangeably long vowels.

unchangeably long vowels. *n.* BH vowels that refuse reduction. Examples in BH and BA are ‏יְ‎, ‏יָ‎, ‏וֹ‎ and ‏וּ‎. GKC §25.

undersubject. *n.* The primary object of a double-accusative construction, as is commonly found with the Hiphil and other causative constructions (e.g., "They elected *him* president").

ungrammatical. *n.* In prescriptive linguistics, any spoken or written *utterance that deviates from the social conventions of the given dialect.

uninflected. *n.* An element of language that does not undergo inflectional change in its usage. Examples of uninflected elements in BH are the *particle of existence ‏יֵשׁ‎ and the particle of nonexistence ‏אַיִן‎.

universals. *n.* Nouns that refer to classes, general qualities, actions and states of being. They are to be distinguished from *particulars, nouns that describe personal or individual things. They are often further distinguished into two other classifications: sortal universals (or just sortals) and characterizing universals. Sortals distribute objects and persons into classes, while characterizing universals comprise such things as abstract nouns, adjectives, verbs and adverbs.

unmarked. *adj.* Referring to a *free morpheme that has not undergone any inflectional or morphological change. *See* markedness.

unmarked order. *n.* The standard BH prose word order (VSO) without the influence of micro- and macrosyntactic modifications. *See also* word order.

unpointed text. *n.* A Hebrew Bible text that lacks the masoretic or other vowel and accent representation systems. These have traditionally been used in the formal synagogue service.

unreal condition. *n.* (1) The circumstances of a *conditional sentence construction that have little to no chance of coming to pass. They are generally considered impossibilities, such as in Jeremiah 33:20-21: *"If you can break my covenant with the day and my covenant with the night, so that day and night will not be at their appointed time, then my covenant may also be broken with my servant David."* (2) The term applies to the volitive moods generally because they identify a state or action that has not yet materialized. (3) The term may also be used with the optative, which conveys a wish or desire without likelihood of fruition.

unvoiced sounds. *See* voiced sounds.

Urdeuteronomium (UrDt). *n.* In biblical criticism, a hypothetical original form of Deuteronomy (or Deuteronomic material) that was successively redacted in later generations to give rise to the final canonical form.

Ur-text. *n.* Any hypothetical document postulated in biblical criticism that supposedly laid the foundation for later and final editions (e.g., *Urdeuteronomium).

utterance. *n.* A sequence of real language communication, whether spoken or in literary form. It is often further defined by linguists as a communication preceded and followed by a silence or pause of some sort.

V

vacillation. *n.* An inconsistency in the spelling of a word in a given language. This may be observed in some Aramaic weak verbs in which sometimes an א will be used instead of a ה or vice versa.

vague referent. *See* neutrum.

valency (verbal). *n.* The way a verb's lexical meaning limits the sentential constituents that it may be used with; also called verbal select. For example, stative verbs will not take a direct or indirect object (e.g., Ps 2:4: יוֹשֵׁב בַּשָּׁמַיִם יִשְׂחָק, "The one who sits in the heavens, *he shall laugh*"). For a *fientive *transitive verb such as *kill*, a direct object is necessary to complete the thought (e.g., Ex 2:14: כַּאֲשֶׁר הָרַגְתָּ אֶת־הַמִּצְרִי, "as you killed the Egyptian").

variable vowel. *See* characteristic vowel.

variant. *n.* In text criticism, the occasion of two or more conflicting manuscript readings for a particular portion of text.

variation. *n.* (1) A change in a language at some point in time. It can be divided further into two subcategories: natural variations and free variations. Natural variations are predictable changes in the language based upon certain established patterns or structural analogy. While most words in English indicate plurality by the *-s* marker (e.g., *boat* becomes *boats)*, certain other words express plurality in unique ways because of pronunciation. As children begin to speak, upon the principle of analogy, they will create such awkward variations such as *tooths* instead of *teeth* or *oxes* instead of *oxen*. Free variations are reflective of sudden and harder-to-explain changes. These may include the creation of new words, the social change in meaning of old words, the dropping of more complicated grammatical constructions and the influences of geography upon a language system. (2) The term also applies to changes in pronunciation from one dialect of a language to another, such as in the case of *systematic correspondence. (3) In semantics, free variation is closely akin to the more traditional term *synonymy. Two words that are interchangeable in a sentence without changing its meaning are said to be in free variation. (4) Allophonic free variation is the interchangeability of *phonemes to different sounds (allophones). For example, the word *either* may be pronounced with the *e* sound in *sea* or with the *i* sound in *kite*.

vassal treaty. *See* treaty.

vav apodosi. *See waw* of apodosis.

vav-**consecutive.** *See waw*-consecutive; *wayyiqtol*.

velar fricative. *See* velars.

velar plosive. *See* velars.

velars. *n.* *Phonemes that are produced by restriction of the upper rear part of the mouth (*velum or soft palate) and may be either a *fricative or a *plosive. They are characterized by a harsh pronunciation, for which reason they have also earned the title emphatic letters (e.g., כ, ח, ק). Some also use the term *velar* loosely to refer to guttural letters.

velum. *n.* The soft upper rear roof of the mouth and the locus for pronunciation of velar sounds (e.g., *k, c* and hard *q*); also called the soft palate.

vellum. *n.* A leather writing material on which *scrolls and *codices were inscribed. A large number of the Dead Sea Scrolls were written on vellum.

verb. *n.* A word that connotes an action or a state of being about the subject of a sentence and fulfills the role of predication in a clause. *See also* fientive verb; stative verb.

verb chain. *n.* A series of finite verbs in BH that are linked by a regular *waw and express a sequence of events. The chain is formed with a regular *waw*-copulative and should not be confused with a *waw*-consecutive sequence.

verb of being. *See* copula.

verb phrase. *See* predicate.

verb sequence. *n.* A series of BH verbs related to one another by use of the **waw*-consecutive. These should not be confused with a *verb chain. *See also* coordinate relationship.

verb stem. *n.* Semitic vowel patterns added to a root that control the verbal voice and mood (e.g., BH Qal, Niphal, Piel). They were traditionally referred to by medieval Hebrew grammarians as **binyanim* (sing. *binyan*, "building"). Joüon §40; MNK §§14-16; GKC §§38-41.

verba abundandi. Lat. "verb of abundance." —*n.* A verb that expresses ideas of fullness, plenty or satisfaction; to be contrasted with **verba deficini.*

verba copiae. See verba abundandi.

verba deficini. Lat. "verb of deficit." —*n.* A verb that expresses ideas of privation or deficiency; to be contrasted with **verba abundandi.*

verba derivative. See derived conjugations.

verba exuendi. n. Lat. "verb of unveiling." —*n.* A verb that expresses ideas of uncovering, unveiling or exposure; to be contrasted with **verba induendi.*

verba induendi. Lat. "verb of adornment." —*n.* A verb that expresses an idea of clothing, putting on or enclosure; to be contrasted with **verba exuendi.*

verbal. *adj.* A broad linguistic classification of anything that functions as a verb. *See also* nominal; nonfinite verb.

verbal adjective. *See* nonfinite verb.

verbal aspect. *See* aspect.

verbal clause. *n.* A clause using any type of finite verb for predication. Verbal clauses are to be contrasted with *nominal clauses, which have nominal predication. Joüon §155; MNK §12; GKC §§140, 142; *IBHS* §4.

verbal complement. *n.* Any sentence element used to clarify the meaning of the verb; any adverbial. For example, in "I am not able to help them," the subject is "I," the verb is "able," the verbal complement is the infinitive phrase "to help them." In English grammar, a verbal complement is to be distinguished from an infinitive as a direct object (e.g., "I am not able *to help*").

verbal hendiadys. *n.* The coordination of two verbs together in which the first serves to clarify the meaning of the second (e.g., Gen 45:13: וּמִהַרְתֶּם וְהוֹרַדְתֶּם אֶת־אָבִי הֵנָּה, "*and you shall expedi-*

tiously bring my father down here"; lit. "and you shall hurry and you shall bring my father down here").

verbal inflection. *See* inflection.

verbal noun. *See* nonfinite verb.

verbal predicate. *n.* A predicate that has a finite verb to express predication. It is to be contrasted with a *predicate nominative.

verbal select. *See* valency (verbal).

verbless clause. *See* nominal clause.

vernacular. *n.* Commonly spoken language with its loose expressions and lack of emphasis on strict rules of grammar and syntax.

verset. *See* colon.

vetitive. *adj.* Expressing prohibition (negative command). This is done in BH by the use of a negative particle and the *jussive.

victory song. *n.* A BH poetic genre that celebrates and extols victory in battle or triumph over one's enemy (e.g., Ex 15; Judg 5; and 1 Sam 18:7).

virtual lengthening. *n.* The ability of some guttural letters to possess a form of weak gemination in pronunciation. *See also* implicit doubling; doubling.

vocal *shewa.* *n.* A half-vowel represented in the MT as two vertically aligned dots ( ). It is identical in form to *silent *shewa* but represents a quick *e* vocalization. As a half-vowel, vocal *shewa* is never to be regarded as forming a syllable of its own, but must always accompany a full vowel. It also has three compound counterparts called *hateph* vowels or compound *shewa*s. It always begins a syllable and is thus found in the following situations: (1) at the beginning of a word; (2) after a syllable with a long vowel; (3) the second of two *shewa*s in a row; (4) after an accented open syllable. It is worth noting that when a *shewa* is found under a doubled consonant, it also represents a doubled value, the first being a silent syllable closer and the second as vocal. Joüon §8; MNK §8.1; GKC §10. *See also* silent *shewa*; compound *shewa*.

vocales impurae. *n.* An archaic term for a long vowel that is not followed by a vowel letter (*mater lectionis) where normally it would be expected. For example, the vowel *tsere* without the vowel-letter *yod* (i.e., ｡ instead of ˙｡) was formally termed a *vocales impurae*. It must be understood that the nomenclature is generally no longer accepted.

vocalic afformative. *See* vocalic sufformative.

vocalic sufformative. *n.* A pronominal suffix that consists of a vowel with no consonants (e.g.,ֹ or ֹ). *See also* heavy consonantal suffix; light consonantal suffix.

vocalization. *n.* The particular pronunciation of the Semitic word with its vowels. Because these languages were alphabetically written without vowels, in many cases the "proper vocalization" becomes a matter of debate.

vocative. *n.* The grammatical case of direct address; also called the nominative of direct address. The vocative is similar to a nominative absolute in that it grammatically stands outside the sentence construction. It is an interjection and throws emphasis upon a second-person pronominal subject (e.g., "James, [you] listen to me!"). Joüon §34.4.

voice. *n.* (1) In traditional grammar, the feature of the verb that defines the relationship of the subject to the predicate, whether *active, middle/*reflexive or *passive. An active verb denotes a subject who is committing the action, a passive voice a subject who is being acted upon and a middle/reflexive voice a subject that is acting upon itself. (2) In modern linguistics in the subdiscipline of *phonetics, the term refers to the vibration of the speaker's vocal cords in pronunciation.

voiced sounds. *n.* The vibration or hum in the vocal cords that is produced in pronouncing certain phonemes. For example, the letter *z* is voiced, but the letter *s* is voiceless (unvoiced). Vowels are generally voiced, while consonants may be either voiced or voiceless.

voiceless. *See* voiced sounds.

volatilization. *n.* The reduction of a full vowel into a *hateph* vowel (half-vowel) in the process of *morphology.

volitional. *adj.* Pertaining to a wish. *See* volitive moods.

volitive. *adj.* Pertaining to a wish. *See* volitive moods.

volitive moods. *n.* Verbal moods or conjugations that express modal aspect such as the *imperative, *jussive *energic and *cohortative. Joüon §§45, 46, 48, 114; MNK §15.3-5; GKC §§46, 48, 108-110; *IBHS* §34

voluntative mood. *See* volitive moods.

Vorlage. Germ. "lying before." —*n.* An *Ur-text or source document that provided the foundation for a later *recension.

vowel. *n.* In traditional grammar, the term *vowel,* like its counterpart *consonant,* is taken for granted; to linguists, a vowel is a voiced sound that is characterized by an outward flow of air. Vowels are further classified in terms of closed versus open (which tells the degree to which the mouth is left open); front versus back (which designates where the sound is articulated); and rounded versus unrounded (which describes the positioning of the lips). GKC §§7-8.

vowel gradation. *n.* The change in vowels according to a particular type of sound; in BH, change within a phonetic family. GKC §9t.

vowel harmony. *n.* The agreement or ease of pronunciation of vowels in successive syllables.

vowel indicators. *See* vowel letters.

vowel letters. *n.* The elements of a premasoretic vowel representation system in which the three Hebrew consonants ‏י‎, ‏ו‎, ‏ה‎ and occasionally ‏א‎ were used as vowel representatives. Joüon §7; GKC §7.

vowel patterns. *n.* The patterns of vowels used with Semitic root words to compose various types of nouns and verbs. They are further classified into simple patterns, which are only composed of vowels themselves, and extended patterns, which include consonantal afformatives.

vowel pointing. *n.* The sublinear system of vowel representation developed by the early rabbinic textual scholars known as the Naqdamim and later analyzed by the Masoretes. The system was developed to preserve the proper *vocalization of the *consonantal text.

vowel quantity. *n.* The particular strength of a vowel, whether long or short.

vowel reduction. *See* pretonic reduction; propretonic reduction.

W

waw **of apodosis.** *n.* A *waw* that is used to join the subordinate clause (*protasis) to the main clause (*apodosis) of a conditional sentence. In such cases, the force of the *waw* is either "then" or "therefore."

waw-**conjunctive.** *n.* A *waw* that is prefixed to a word and used as a conjunction (e.g., *and, then, also, now* or *but*). A conjunctive *waw* may be further distinguished as a word-level *waw* and a clause-level *waw*. The word-level *waw* joins words, while the clause-level *waw* joins and relates clauses. GKC §154.

waw-consecutive. *n.* A *waw*-relative plus a finite verb form to create a verbal sequence. The *waw* plus imperfect *(*wayyiqtol)* forms the backbone of BH historical narrative. Joüon §§117-120; MNK §21; GKC §§111-112; *IBHS* §§32-33. See *waw*-relative.

waw-conservative. *See* waw-consecutive.

waw-conversive. *See* waw-consecutive.

waw-copulative. *n.* A clause-level *waw* that relates a sequence of verbs into a discourse unit known as a *verb chain; often used as another term for *waw*-conjunctive. It is to be distinguished from *waw*-consecutive in that while it relates the verbs in sequence it does not affect verbal aspect (perfect versus imperfect). *See also* waw-conjunctive.

waw-disjunctive. *n.* A clause-level *waw* that creates a disjunction between two clauses (e.g., Gen 13:12: אַבְרָם יָשַׁב בְּאֶרֶץ־כְּנָעַן וְלוֹט יָשַׁב עָרֵי הַכִּכָּר, "Abram dwelt in the land of Canaan, *but* Lot dwelt among the cities of the valley").

waw-inversive. See *waw*-consecutive.

waw-relative. *n.* A more contemporary and linguistically informed choice in terminology for what was traditionally called the *waw*-consecutive or *waw*-conversive. This choice in terminology seeks to emphasize that the *waw*, marking the opening of a new clause, relates its action to the previous and so on. The term is used for both the *weqatal* and *wayyiqtol* conjugations. *IBHS* §§32-33.

waw-resultative. See *waw*-consecutive.

wayyiqtol. *n.* The *waw*-consecutive plus imperfect verbal sequence that forms the backbone of Hebrew narrative; also known as the narrative tense. It is also referred to as the mainline or online verb form, in contrast to offline prose sequences, which do not carry the main narration but provide background information. A series of *wayyiqtol* verbs are most often begun by a perfect verb form to construct a narration referring to past or historical events, but this is only a general rule. Joüon §§47, 117-120; GKC §§48, 111-112; *IBHS* §§32-33; MNK §21. *See also* waw-consecutive; *waw*-relative; imperfect.

weak letters. *n.* In narrow terms it refers to *waw* and *yod*, which are also known as semivowels. More broadly it refers to letters that drop or assimilate. GKC §24, §§6s, 19b-l.

weak verb. *n.* A verb that deviates from the normal verbal patterns because it has a guttural letter, a quiescent letter or a letter such as נ or ל, which commonly assimilate; also called an irregular verb. Weak verbs are characterized by the unstable nature of one of the three root consonants.

weakening. *n.* The softening of a consonantal sound for smoothing of pronunciation. *Begadkepat* letters undergo weakening (*aspiration) when the *dagesh lene* is omitted because the letter follows an *open syllable.

weqatal. *n.* The *waw-consecutive* plus perfect verbal sequence that changes or "converts" the function of the perfect verb to the force of an imperfect or, at times, volitive. The *waw*-consecutive of the *qatal* does not differ in form from a regular *waw*-conjunctive (וְ) and thus must be identified according to context. A series of *weqatal* verbs will often be preceded by a regular *imperfect verb form to establish a narration of incomplete events. The narrative use is usually descriptive, predictive or prescriptive. *See also waw*-consecutive. Joüon §§43, 117-120; GKC §§48, 111-112; *IBHS* §§32-33; MNK §21.

West Aramaic. *See* Aramaic.

wisdom literature. *n.* (1) In *literary and *genre criticism, *sapential writing; (2) more specifically, the books of Job, Proverbs, Ecclesiastes and the Song of Songs in the Hebrew canon.

wishes. *See* volitive moods.

word. *n.* The most rudimentary unit of semantic signification. Theoretical linguists consider a word to be a sign or *signifier that points to any *animate, *inanimate or *abstract entity (the *signified). They also distinguish between *full words, which have independent meaning apart from sentential relations, and *form or *function words, which only have meaning in relation to full words as they are placed into *syntagms. *See also* signification.

word chain. *See* syntagm.

word class. *See* parts of speech.

word divider. *n.* One of various forms of marking (usually a dot or vertical stroke) found in many ancient epigraphic remains to separate words for clarity in reading.

word group. *n.* A *phrase or *syntagm.

word order. *n.* The conventions of any given language that dictate the order of words and syntactical constitution. The import of word order differs from language to language. While it is never completely unimportant to a language, Greek and Aramaic are quite flexible, in contrast to BH, in which it is critical.

word pair. *n.* In the study of discourse semantics, a linguistic classification for pairs of words that have a certain special relationship to one another. These can especially include *synonyms and *antonyms (e.g., *good* and *bad*; *beast* and *creeping thing*; *righteous* and *wicked*). Word pairs are most often identified by their common occurrence together, especially in BH poetry, where they serve as a building block of Hebrew parallelism.

word sense. *n.* The lexical range of meaning a single word can have in all its possible contexts, the so-called *semantic field; to be contrasted with *discourse sense.

word-final. *adj.* Referring to a *bound morpheme, accent or anything placed at the end of a word.

word-initial. *adj.* Referring to a *bound morpheme, accent or anything placed at the beginning of a word.

word-medial. *adj.* Referring to a *bound morpheme, accent or anything placed in the middle of a word.

wordplay. *n.* The creative use of words in relation to one another to produce multiple connotations, as in the case of *double entendre.

Writings. *See* Ketubim.

X

x-question. *n.* Any question not using a *wh-* form, such as "Do you know him?" as opposed to a *wh-* form "Who is he?"

x // x + y phenomenon. *n.* A BH parallelism structure in which a word in the first colon is followed by the same word plus a modifier in the second colon, such as in Song 1:10-11:

x (תרים‎) // x (תורי‎) + y (זהב‎).

Y

Yavneh. *See* Jamnia.

Yiddish. *n.* A composite language formed of medieval Hebrew and German and used among the traditional Jewish communities of Northern Europe; also referred to as Judeo-German.

yiqtol **conjugation.** *See* imperfect.

Z

zero morpheme. *n.* An inflection or declension implied by the absence of a morpheme. In the BH perfect conjugation, all forms have *sufformatives to indicate person, gender and number except for the third masculine singular. The lack of markedness is in fact its markedness, which is called a zero morph.

zero-marked form. *See* zero morpheme.